Praise for *Confessions of a Bad Teacher*

"If poor city and suburban schools had more 'bad' teachers like John Owens, they'd be much more places of dreams than despair. Teachers are on the front line of respect—and deserve to be—in 'The System.'"

—Lawrence Levy, Dean, National Center for
Suburban Studies, at Hofstra University

"*Confessions of a Bad Teacher* is hyperbole as a title but dead-on in its characterizations, and reveals the weaknesses of the criticisms, the true fault-lines in public education, and the nobility of a profession being treated unfairly."

—Dr. Robert A. Scott, President, Adelphi University

"A compelling and thoughtful personal narrative about corporate school reform's war on teachers."

—Michael Klonsky, PhD, DePaul University

"This book is *Freedom Writers* meets *One Flew Over the Cuckoo's Nest.* Inspiring and heartbreaking."

—Angela Susan Anton, Publisher, Anton (Long Island)
Community Newspapers, New York

"*Confessions of a Bad Teacher* by John Owens is a vivid account of life in the corporate school reform trenches, with all the agony, comedy, hope, and humiliation experienced by so many of today's public school teachers. Owens goes beyond telling war stories to reflect on the big picture of bad policies and politics that drive the school day, and to offer some steps readers can take to preserve and protect the precious gift of democratic public education."

—Julie Woestehoff, cofounder, Parents Across America

"John Owens's *Confessions of a Bad Teacher* offers a devastating portrait of the utter failure of the school reform movement at ground zero: the school, the classroom, and the teacher under assault."

—Norm Scott, founding member of the
Independent Community of Educators

"Here's the soul-wrenching scoop on what happens when a middle-aged professional who's great with kids, loves literature, and wants to 'give back' decides to become a teacher. Being willing to work from 5 a.m. to 10 p.m. is not enough in the face of a broken system that includes a crazy principal. This is a book every urban teacher can relate to and everybody else should read."

—Susan Ohanian, author of *What Happened to Recess* and
Why Are Our Children Struggling in Kindergarten?

"Our media has found an easy scapegoat in America's teachers.... An antidote to such propaganda, *Confessions of a Bad Teacher* by John Owens gives readers an insight into the conditions in which too many of America's teachers work—discouraging and disparaging.... Owens writes as one who has been there, and his veracity at once discourages and inspires; he has given a voice to teachers, a voice that parents and the polis need to hear."

—Dr. Joseph D'Angelo, Fellow, Teacher of the Year, Harvard Club

CONFESSIONS OF A BAD TEACHER

The Shocking Truth
from the Front Lines of
American Public Education

JOHN OWENS

§ sourcebooks

Published by Sourcebooks, Inc.
P.O. Box 4410, Naperville, Illinois 60567-4410
(630) 961-3900
Fax: (630) 961-2168
www.sourcebooks.com

Library of Congress Cataloging-in-Publication Data is on file with the publisher.

Printed and bound in the United States of America.
VP 10 9 8 7 6 5 4 3 2 1

10/6/14

For Aidan and Demetria

CONTENTS

INTRODUCTION

Will non-English-speaking students start speaking English because their teachers were fired? Will children come to school ready to learn because their teachers were fired?

Since we can't fire poverty, we can't fire students, and we can't fire families, all that is left is to fire teachers.

—Diane Ravitch, Former U.S. Assistant Secretary of Education,
Author of *The Death and Life of the Great American School System:*
How Testing and Choice are Undermining Education

AFTER WE READ THE section of Homer's *The Odyssey* where Odysseus and his men confront the Cyclops, we watched a movie clip of how the clever Greek hero blinded that wine-swilling, man-eating, one-eyed monster and escaped. We discussed the story for a while, and I then asked my eighth-grade class to break up into groups and write down various plot points. After about ten minutes, we reviewed the points out loud.

The kids loved the blood, bellowing, running around, and sailing away. But there was a lot of confusion about who was who and what was going on. In other words, a lot of the students were having a tough time figuring out the story. So I set to work helping them figure it out. After all, it's hard to understand the significance of a story if you don't understand the story itself.

The assistant principal, who was observing the class, later scolded me for the lesson's "lack of academic rigor." Instead of merely "identifying" what was going on, he believed we should have been working higher up the cognitive food chain by "analyzing," "differentiating," and "inferring" everything from motivations to psychological states of the characters.

Yet the assistant principal knew as well as I did that at least one of these eighth graders could barely read. Alfred, a thirteen-year-old recent immigrant from Ghana, would smile brightly whenever I glanced his way and pop out of his seat proudly, standing straight and tall next to his desk, whenever he answered a question. But reading comprehension was another matter.

One day during lunch, I pulled him aside and gave him some fourth-grade reading material and multiple-choice questions about the text to get a basic sense of his reading level. "How was that?" I asked.

"Easy," Alfred responded, smiling. "Easy."

But looking at the answers he had circled on the quiz, I could see that he had no idea what the material said. Each day Alfred handed in homework, but it never was related to the assignment; it was merely a neatly copied version of what I had presented the day before on the whiteboard or Smart Board.* On tests and quizzes, Alfred copied whatever was on the paper of the student next

---

*The whiteboard is an updated version of the old classroom blackboard or greenboard. Instead of chalk, it uses felt-tipped markers. The Smart Board takes the whiteboard into the world of computers, projectors, software, and interactive displays. Developed by SMART Technologies, a Smart Board is like a giant touchscreen computer that can show videos, access the Internet, be written on with "digital ink," and respond to the user's touch.

to him and smiled brightly whenever I gave him a look of "What are you doing?"

All of his other teachers had the same experience with Alfred, and the principal told us to get together and figure out how to bring him up to speed in our "spare time." In fact, whenever there was an issue with a student who was far behind or had a behavior problem, we were told to handle the situation in our spare time. Unfortunately, with his good behavior and smiling demeanor, Alfred often fell to the back of the line as his teachers performed triage in dealing with the problems at hand.

The assistant principal also was aware that some of my students had other obvious special needs and learning disabilities, which were largely ignored or undiagnosed. One student, Siah, spent most of the forty-six-minute period punching the students around him and sticking objects into various orifices of his body. Bigger and taller than the other eighth graders, Siah was a loveable bear of a kid, with a striking resemblance to the rapper Drake and what seemed like a serious case of attention deficit hyperactivity disorder (ADHD). When he entered my class at the end of the day, his school uniform was blotched with sweat, ink, and the remains of major and minor food fights throughout the day. His shirttails were out, and his tie was loose and flapping like a pennant carried by the color guard of a battle-weary regiment.

Despite seven previous periods of punching, throwing, running, shouting, backpack-swinging, and desk-pounding, by the time he joined my class for eighth period, Siah typically was still raring to go. If another kid wasn't goading him by stealing his backpack and stuffing it in the trash can, or challenging him to a human beatbox contest ("Siah, you go first"), he had his neck craned as he searched the classroom for some action, the way an English pointer searches for a pheasant. And it was rare for him to not find it.

Siah was among the students with obvious special-education needs in my eighth-period class. From what I could figure, at least eight of the twenty-eight kids had learning or behavior or emotional problems that meant they were entitled—by law—to assistance, guidance, and, typically, medication.* But dealing with these students as the law required would have meant employing a school nurse and many more special-education teachers. And not only are qualified special-ed teachers in short supply, but also the low student-teacher ratio required by following the rules would eat up the school's budget. So, instead of directly addressing the problems of these kids, the administration made the students' problems the classroom teachers' problem, pretending that they weren't really special-education students at all.

The assistant principal knew that the two groups of girls who actually did what I asked—make a list of plot points in the scene—had a tough time getting them straight. They were earnest in their attempts but confused about chronology and who did what. Even for these "good students," paying close attention and

---

*In the United States, approximately 9 percent of all children have been diagnosed with attention deficit hyperactivity disorder (ADHD), according to a 2011 report from the National Center for Health Statistics. Among poor kids, the rate is even higher: 10 percent for children with family income less than 100 percent of the poverty level and 11 percent for those with family income between 100 and 199 percent of the poverty level. (http://www.cdc.gov/nchs/data/data briefs/db70.htm)

As in school districts around the country, New York City's special-ed landscape is full of rules, requirements, and exceptions. The city offers a guide to the general terrain in the regularly updated, downloadable book, *A Parent's Guide to Special Education Services for School-Age Children*. (http://schools.nyc .gov/NR/rdonlyres/DBD4EB3A-6D3B-496D-8CB2-C742F9B9AB5C/0/ ParentGuidetoSpecialEd_090712_English.pdf)

simply describing what happened in the story wasn't part of their academic toolkit.

The assistant principal also knew that only Santos was far ahead of the rest of the class. When Santos discovered we were going to cover *The Odyssey*, he read all he could find on the topic in the class textbook and online. The son of Hispanic immigrants, Santos was tall and thin, and wore thick glasses. Bright, eager, and ready with the correct answer to every question ever asked, Santos was the perfect student. He deserved to be attending one of New York City's elite public schools, but his parents, who didn't speak English, didn't press for a transfer. Instead, he was in my class in the South Bronx at the troubled, dysfunctional public school I call Latinate Institute.

Although Santos was ready for an in-depth discussion of *The Odyssey*, most of the rest of the class was still trying to figure out what the Greeks were doing in the Cyclops' cave in the first place or silently taunting kids across the room by mouthing "Suck my dick, nigga!"*

But I knew better than to challenge the assistant principal's assessment. I had done that before and been shot down. Trying to get some help for Siah's ADHD (which would benefit not only him, but also his classmates and me) simply led to the assistant principal's suggestion that Siah was acting up because I wasn't sufficiently challenging the writer within him. It was the same with a ninth-grade girl who was pleasant and cooperative one

---

*Like all profanity, "the N word" was forbidden at Latinate Institute. Yet for many of the students, its use was as natural and regular as respiration. Both black and Hispanic students made it central to their vocabulary, using it to refer to a close friend ("My nigga!"), an enemy ("Fuck you, nigga!"), a random individual ("That nigga almost got hit by a bus!"), or a collective body ("Damn! All the other niggas did the homework!").

day, violent and disruptive the next, with the pattern alternating every few days.

"Oh, no. She is a very good student," the assistant principal assured me, waving the issue and me away with a flutter of his hand.

The principal and assistant principal were quite clear that Latinate was a model of school reform, and I quickly realized we teachers were there to enforce that idea. As the principal saw it, all of the problems of a traditional public school in a high-needs area—low student achievement, wildly inappropriate behavior, and a high concentration of special-needs students—would be overcome by the teachers following and enforcing the principal's various mission statements, vision statements, expectations, non-negotiables, and other assorted Big Ideas.

If I pressed the issue of Alfred being unable to read, I would have been told that if I were a good teacher, I would spend as much time as necessary with Alfred improving his skills. If I again brought up the issue of Siah and his ADHD and the need for a school nurse to administer his medication, I would have been told that if I were a good teacher, I would be able to "engage" him with interesting work or use "the force of my personality" to at least make him—and the other twenty-seven kids in the class—sit quietly for the forty-six-minute period.

And if I raised the issue of Santos being so far ahead of the rest of the class that it wasn't fair to keep him here, I would have been told that if I were a good teacher, every lesson and assignment I presented would span the wide range of academic skills among the students. Or, more accurately, each lesson every day would be tailored to each of my 125 students' individual needs—targeting every gradation between illiterate and near-college—and revised constantly. For me, it wasn't just difficult, it was impossible. From 5 a.m. to 10 p.m. every day during my teaching career,

I was consumed with the work of teaching. It was as though I had just joined the circus as an apprentice clown and was immediately required to juggle plates, bowling pins, butcher's knives, and axes all day long while walking along a tightrope in midair.

Clearly, I wasn't a good teacher. In fact, the assistant principal had "proof"—file folders bulging with observation reports and other alleged evidence that any shortcomings in my students' academics or behavior were solely my fault. At Latinate Institute, as in schools across the country, all problems apparently boiled down to one simple cause: bad teachers like me.

America's public school teachers are being loudly and unfairly blamed for the failure of our nation's public schools. From Bill Gates, to hedge-fund-enriched charter school backers, to New York City Mayor Michael Bloomberg, to an endless stream of reports in the media, everyone "knows" that we must fix the Bad Teacher problem.

If only teachers were better…smarter…more committed to their students. If only they had a longer workday and a longer school year. If only they didn't have tenure. If only they didn't have such powerful unions. If only they didn't stand in the way of progress.

Today, *all* teachers seem to be considered bad until proven otherwise. Campaigns for school reform and corporate-style management of our public schools are sweeping the country. As a result, individual principals have been given a stunning amount of power and leeway to decide who's a good teacher and who's a bad teacher. With that much authority in the hands of a few top administrators who have little accountability for their decisions, it's easy for good management and honest evaluation of teachers to be trampled during administrators' efforts to deliver stellar results in unrealistically short periods of time.

On top of that, precisely what defines a "bad teacher" isn't clear. There are too many factors—from standardized test scores to subjective department evaluations—and the criteria vary from state to state, school district to school district. But from what I've seen, unless a teacher turns in grades and standardized test scores in the highest level of academic achievement while the students perform in class as the educational equivalents of the von Trapp kids in *The Sound of Music*, there's a chance of being branded a bad teacher. Too many of America's schools are run on the belief that everything would be great if not for these bad teachers. Today, the term seems to be used almost interchangeably with the word "teachers" itself.

This must change. The bad teacher witch-hunt is destroying our schools and robbing our children of their future. My experience on the front lines of education has brought me to the conclusion that America's public school policies are drowning children, not helping them. Many good, well-intentioned, and truly effective educators across the country are reaching, stretching, trying desperately to save these kids, but those in charge increasingly beat them back, insisting that these teachers are not using the appropriate method of rescue. Meanwhile, the children are carried off downstream, flailing.

This is not an exaggeration. Throughout the country, we are told that everything we have been doing in our schools is wrong. The education system that once was the envy of the world has become a hopeless, costly, out-of-control dinosaur.

Further, we hear that the only way to save American education is through school reform—to manage our schools as though they were businesses, employing powerful, hard-nosed leaders who make tough rules and use data to measure students' progress and teachers' accountability in order to punish those who impede success. This version of school reform is rooted in the appealing notion of using scientific studies to determine what's needed and how to fix it. A 2002 report from the U.S. Department of Education's Office of Elementary and Secondary Education envisioned school reform this way:

> The primary responsibility of schools undertaking comprehensive school reform is creating programs that result in improved student achievement. One of the most important tasks in this process is choosing highly effective reform strategies, methods, and programs, those that are grounded in scientifically based research.

But these days, "scientifically based research" has been replaced by "data"—test scores, class grades, and, as I saw, virtually any number that can be recorded and crunched.

The current version of school reform, as championed by those such as Jeb Bush, the former Florida governor and now chairman of the Foundation for Excellence in Education, has a common-sense ring to it with mantras such as "put students first, support effective teachers, and continue to hold everyone accountable for results."

But the more subtle and much more important point is that all too often Bush and others like him replace "scientifically based research" and "highly effective reform strategies, methods, and programs" with data-driven grades for schools and data-driven rewards and punishments for teachers. As Bush put it in a 2011 article on Politico.com:

> A–F systems [for grading schools] are more intuitive to parents and the public. They also help leaders to clearly

> differentiate rewards and interventions for schools....
> Many states and school districts are now adopting more
> advanced data systems, linking student performance
> to teachers. For the first time, we can measure teacher
> effectiveness using transparent objectives and standards.

It's a data-driven solution that speaks of efficiency and the digital genius that has built technology powerhouses such as Microsoft and Google and made billionaires of hedge-fund managers. But it masks the real truth.

We see the success stories in films such as *Waiting for "Superman,"* which portrays teachers' unions as venal, data-averse impediments to better schools and casts "reformers" as visionary leaders heroically struggling to overcome the forces of self-interest that are holding children back.

We also hear how charter schools produce amazing results. Released from some of the rules, regulations, and statutes that apply to other public schools, charter schools often are free to extend the usual school day by several hours, require weekend classes, and demand extensive parental involvement. Charter schools are often independent—sometimes for-profit—operations that, at least in the public imagination, are managed by tough, visionary leaders who gain the freedom to run the school *their way* in exchange for accountability in producing results.

But the brilliance, easy answers, and immediate measurable results of school reform have not been proven. Studies going back nearly a decade conflict with the popular image of the magically successful charter school. In December 2004, the National Assessment of Educational Progress (NAEP) released research showing that fourth-grade charter school students do no better than their public school counterparts on math and reading assessments, and in some cases score lower. A 2009 sixteen-state study of charter schools by Stanford University's Center for Research on Education Outcomes (CREDO) turned up a similarly mixed bag, heavy on disappointing results:

> The group portrait shows wide variation in performance. The study reveals that a decent fraction of charter schools, 17 percent, provide superior education opportunities for their students. Nearly half of the charter schools nationwide have results that are no different from the local public school options and over a third, 37 percent, deliver learning results that are significantly worse than their students would have realized had they remained in traditional public schools.

While the CREDO study is—so far—the gold standard on the topic, headlines from the industry publication *Education Week* also vividly demonstrate the confused and quite often lackluster state of charter school achievement:

- "Study Finds No Clear Edge for Charter Schools" (June 29, 2010).
- "KIPP Middle Schools [Charter Schools] Found to Spur Learning Gains" (June 22, 2010).
- "Study Casts Doubt on Strength of Charter Managers" (December 3, 2009; updated April 4, 2012).
- "Study Casts Doubt on Charter School Results" (June 15, 2009).

Proponents of charter schools and school reform, politicians, and business leaders dismiss these dubious results with one explanation. The reason charter schools and school reform haven't been an unqualified success is simple, they say. It's because there are so many bad teachers, and we can't get rid of them fast enough.

The truth, of course, is not so simple. Teachers have become scapegoats for a broken system that isn't being fixed, but rather is being gradually destroyed. The real problem, it seems, is that with so many issues plaguing our educational system, blaming teachers is easier than doing a massive system overhaul. As a result, many of our public schools have been put in the hands of "visionary managers" who insist that strictly enforced procedures and data-driven business principles will revitalize American education.

But as dozens of test-score-manipulation scandals from Atlanta to Los Angeles to Washington, D.C., have proven, all too often these administrators are neither visionaries nor managers. They are, in many cases, misguided or tyrannical number-crunchers who use their skills with spreadsheets and theatrics to make parents and taxpayers believe that our children are being educated—and educated well, at that—when in fact, they are just bit players in a giant pageant of data and window dressing.

Along the way, these administrators secure their power by demonizing the people closest to our children, their teachers. Consider, for instance, Michelle Rhee, one of the most famous proponents of school reform. The student achievement numbers she's reported from her own teaching career have been questioned, and while chancellor of the Washington, D.C., public schools, she fired 266 teachers who, she claimed, "had hit children, who had had sex with children, who had missed seventy-eight days of school." (The statement appeared in the February 2010 issue of the business magazine *Fast Company*.)

When pressed to back up her claims, Rhee "clarified" that actually only one teacher was dismissed due to sexual abuse allegations, and she didn't address the other issues. Teachers' union officials pointed out that Rhee presented no evidence for her charges. Still, the damage was done. Meanwhile, Rhee, despite her record of suspect data and unnecessarily vilifying teachers, remains a powerful, listened-to voice in American education.

But why believe me? I'm a bad teacher.

According to my personnel file at the New York City Department of Education, I am "unprofessional," "insubordinate," and "culturally insensitive." I can't maintain order in the classroom, and even when I do establish order, I can't properly explain the lesson. As if that's not enough, I tend to place students in a "dangerous and unsafe situation," and I might be a racist.

Mind you, I didn't set out to be a "bad teacher." When I left a high-level publishing job in a Manhattan skyscraper to teach English at a public school in New York City's South Bronx, I thought I could do some good for underprivileged kids. I am a middle-aged professional, but I'm not lazy. I'm not crazy. I'm great with kids and I love literature.

My love of words has taken me from a troubled, working-class childhood to a wonderfully happy, successful life. I have been writing—and teaching others to write—for a long time. And I have enjoyed helping younger writers build great careers. During a three-decade career as a writer, editor, and corporate executive, I had traveled to more than a hundred countries, met heads of state, and picked up some wisdom about getting along and getting ahead in life that I thought was worth sharing with those just starting the journey. I wanted to make an impact directly with kids in the classroom. To use the cliché, I felt it was time to "give back."

There was something else at work here, too. For want of a

better word, I will call it patriotism. The flood of immigrants into New York City in recent years has been astounding. Currently, nearly 40 percent of the city's residents are immigrants, according to data compiled by the Weissman Center for International Business at Baruch College. Queens and Manhattan have seen huge influxes from China. The Bronx and Brooklyn are teeming with Dominicans. Africans, especially from the central belt of the continent, are numerous in the Bronx. Needless to say, the children who have come with or been born to these recent arrivals are the future of our country. They need teachers and mentors, guides to help them navigate what often is a new world. Teachers like the ones I had growing up. Teachers who can present a passion for the greatness and potential of learning and the greatness and potential of America. Teachers who can make kids want to be upstanding, successful Americans.

The school where I landed touted itself as a model of school reform. Its website presented a showcase of high standards and a passion for learning. The interview that sealed the job was more about practical concerns than such lofty ideals, but what did it matter? It was the job offer I had clinched, and no matter what, I was determined to help poor kids, immigrant kids, and kids who simply needed people to inspire them, believe in them, and encourage them to succeed.

Instead, I experienced firsthand school reform gone terribly wrong. Students who did nothing were passed, and students who did nothing more than cut and paste from Wikipedia were deemed high performers. Special-needs students were swept along with their classmates while their real problems were swept under the rug. Disruptive students were permitted to rob their classmates of precious teaching time.

Teachers who were skilled, enthusiastic, caring, and hardworking were held accountable for every ill in the school and every problem each student faced, most of which were entirely unrelated to their classes. Some teachers were able to survive the system with luck, savvy, and years of skills to rely on, or with sacrifices to serve the administration's interests, rather than the students'. Some, like me, were not so fortunate. And all because the data could be worked over—or even invented—to give the appearance that the kids were learning and that the principal was indeed a visionary leader.

As common as this is, the media spotlight rarely shines on the schools that are failures of reform. Schools run by tyrannical principals. Schools where the much-vaunted data is easily manipulated. Most importantly, schools where our children aren't getting the education they need. When it was clear that my teaching career was doomed, I decided it was time to bring this issue to light and wrote an article for Salon.com describing my experiences in the Smart Board jungle.

"Confessions of a Bad Teacher" told of my heartfelt efforts— and sometimes successes—at teaching English to eighth- and ninth-grade inner-city kids while a crazed visionary manager (the principal) terrorized the teachers and filled folder after folder with our misdeeds. The article went viral, and Salon's comment section swelled:

> "I'm a teacher, too. This is exactly what it's like working in urban schools."
>
> "Great story. Maybe the best story I've ever read about what it's REALLY like in an urban school (I worked in South Central LA for eight years)."
>
> "Heartrending."
>
> "A beautifully written tragedy."
>
> "At last, a voice of experience."

Thousands of people reached out from all over the country to tell me how much of a major problem this is throughout America. Former U.S. Assistant Secretary of Education and best-selling author Diane Ravitch tweeted my article to her 18,000 followers. MSNBC brought me to its Rockefeller Center studios for a live interview. From blogs to discussion boards to emails I received from readers who tracked me down through LinkedIn, the message was clear: "Confessions of a Bad Teacher" had struck a nerve. It was the truth behind so much of today's school reform.

That's why I wrote this book—to tell the story of this outrage, of this total failure of visionary managers and easy solutions for our broken educational system. Across the nation, in communities of all sizes and at every rung of the economic ladder, hundreds of thousands—perhaps millions—of children are cheated of a real education, and hundreds of thousands of passionate, hard-working, results-oriented educators are demonized and belittled because America is looking for easy fixes.

Another reason for writing this was to explore solutions to our public education woes and offer advice for parents, teachers, students, and anyone else who understands that education truly does represent the future of America. Toward that end, I have included some key facts and figures that illustrate the scope and depth of our national problem, as well as crucial lessons I learned from my time at Latinate and from the hundreds of other educators, administrators, parents, and students I've spoken with since then. And, although I'm supposedly a bad teacher, I also respectfully offer some suggestions to add to our national dialogue.

This is not a book about policy. It's a book about people—primarily the people I taught, taught with, and worked for during my career in education. Each is an individual, though I'm sure there are people much like each of them at schools around America.

As we journey through the school and the education system, you'll meet students, parents, teachers, and administrators and hear their stories. Some are hilarious. Some heartbreaking. There are some dedicated saints and a couple of unmitigated villains. Most, however, are just ordinary people grappling with extraordinary situations. And there are lessons for all of America's parents, educators, and taxpayers in their stories. Among the people you'll meet are:

- Africah, the foul-mouthed, sixteen-year-old, eighth-grade girl who became an odd teacher's pet.
- Rikkie, the tough, snarling ninth grader whose father was serving six years in prison and who just needed a chance to prove that he was smart, perhaps brilliant.
- Cristofer, who fancied himself a fifteen-year-old Puerto Rican tough ("I didn't even cry when my father died"), and found purpose and discipline when entrusted with a classroom job.
- Ms. Lyons, the veteran science teacher whose knack for survival includes such rules as "Never lean against the wall, or the cockroaches will crawl up your back."
- And, of course, Ms. P, the principal and "visionary leader," whose perverse ego and incompetence were combined with a serious case of Crazy Boss syndrome.

You'll also read firsthand reports from other teachers across America and what they face in this era of school reform and bad teachers. My school's situation and mismanagement were terrible—both for the teachers and for the students. Yet the school was not ranked among the worst of the hundreds of high schools in New York City. In some ways, the data placed it in the top tier of city schools. That a school this awful should be highly ranked shows just what a mess we're in.

But there are steps that we as a nation can take to clean up this mess. It must start, of course, with an honest search for answers. And honesty demands that we stop the polarizing bad-teacher witch-hunt, which isn't solving our public education issues. At the same time, we must stop believing in superhero principals and administrators as the quick and easy solution to this problem. They are myths, products of popular imagination. As much as America might want them to, visionary managers are not going to save our students and schools. In fact, from what I've seen, the opposite is true. In today's educational system, not only does power corrupt, but combining power and data corrupts both the person and the data. And that leaves us worse off than ever.

Instead, we need to address directly and honestly the needs of so many of our children both inside and outside the classroom and how those needs affect our ability to educate them and their abilities to learn. And despite what school reformers lead America to believe, no teacher can provide or be responsible for everything every child needs. Only by taking an honest approach to solving the problems can we save the drowning children who are in our public schools.

GOOD-BYE TOO SOON

In urban districts, close to 50 percent of newcomers leave the profession during their first five years of teaching.

—National Commission on Teaching and America's Future

N o! No! It ain't true," Pashima wailed as she ran up the linoleum-tiled hallway to the homeroom door. "Say you ain't leaving us!"

Every other day, Pashima and I stood by the door. I held a clipboard and attempted to note attendance for the ninth graders, who was and wasn't in uniform, and, as they breezed by, who was and wasn't in adherence with the school's core values (a list of traits the students were expected to exhibit, developed by the principal along the lines of the seven heavenly virtues). The clipboard gave me an air of authority, of keeping score, and of knowing to the precise decimal point who was naughty and who was nice, or at least who had properly knotted the school tie and who, while coming to homeroom, was displaying such values as self-determination and unity of being. Alongside me, Pashima surveyed the action in the hall and kept a running commentary on the latest developments at Latinate Institute.[*]

"Yo, Tina. Your hair looks good."

"Oh, Ashley, new shoes. Nice."

Usually perky and relentlessly involved in anything and everything social, 14-year-old Pashima envisioned herself as the Cutest Thing Around. She had a pink phone, pink backpack, pink lipstick, pink ribbons in her pulled-back, lightly processed hair. She took modeling classes on weekends and was convinced she would one day marry Justin Bieber. On the cover of her pink binder she practiced her post-marital signature.

> *Pashima Bieber*
> *Mrs. Pashima Bieber*
> *Pashima, Mrs. Justin Bieber*

…and so forth.

Pashima could have spent the better part of the morning flitting among the groups that formed on the sidewalk outside the school, in the halls outside the girls' restroom, and on the landings of the two primary staircases. But instead, she got up to my third-floor homeroom as early as she could to take her post alongside me.

Today, however, she wasn't perky. The future Mrs. Bieber's eyes were red and her cheeks moist as she looked at me.

"No, man, don't go," said Mark, following Pashima into the classroom. He was shaking his head and contorting his mouth into a grimace of disappointment. At nearly six and half feet, this ninth

---

[*]The name of the school has been changed, as have the names of the children and adults, along with identifying details.

grader towered over me, and I felt especially small as he passed by me and muttered, "We need you."

A South Bronx all-American kid (his grandparents had immigrated from Jamaica), Mark exuded a well-mannered self-confidence. His mother kept a close eye on him and his studies; I recalled she came to parent-teacher night directly from her shift at the post office. Good at sports, knowledgeable about music, Mark was also an engaging rapper when he wasn't studying or raising his hand to answer every question in class. ("Oh, I was in middle school with Mark, and he's such a brain," an admiring girl told me.)

"Damn. It's not right," said Michael, with an intensity usually reserved for talking about the Dominican Republic or Yankee baseball. Growing fast as the hormones of puberty raced through him, Michael had the start of a moustache on his upper lip and a wiry frame that was roaring toward six feet.

"Michael, the hat," I said, nodding in the direction of his Yankees cap.

He took it off, glowered at me, and waved the hat violently, as though I had forced him to donate a kidney without anesthesia, though, in fact, we had gone through this hat-removal ritual every day since school began.

I had planned to make my last day as a teacher quiet and uneventful. My career had lasted less than a year and the principal, Ms. P, considered me such a bad teacher that not only did she have file folders bursting with evidence of my pedagogical shortcomings, but there also was a lingering threat that she would have me arrested at any moment for what she characterized as an incident of "corporal punishment," when I tried to keep my eighth graders after school as detention for their severe misbehavior.

Under this pressure, I had finally resigned my teaching post and accepted a new job in my former profession, publishing. I figured I would slip out of Latinate Institute in New York City's South Bronx and fade into the large and ever-growing ranks of teachers purged and pushed out of a system that, if conventional wisdom is to be believed, is awash in bad teachers who are sucking up our tax dollars and fettering our children's future.

To make my departure as low-key as possible, I hadn't told the kids ahead of time. I didn't want to seem insensitive, but I knew that lots of advance notice wouldn't help their behavior and classwork. The only thing worse than a lame teacher is a lame-duck teacher. I had planned to tell the kids on the last day. But somehow they found out beforehand.

"Did we get you in too much trouble?" Michael asked, looking at me seriously.

"No," I said dismissively. "I'm leaving because Ms. P doesn't like my work. You guys have been great."

But I knew he was thinking about the recent visit from an administrator who came into class and scolded me for giving Michael after-school detention nearly a dozen times without calling his mother.

"Oh, I didn't know I had to call his mother," I said sheepishly, thinking back to meeting Michael's father at parent-teacher night. He had come in clothes covered in the gray dust of concrete work, and his son provided the English-Spanish translation as I praised the young man's effort and both father and son smiled proudly. A call didn't seem like it would help much, especially to a mother who didn't speak English and might interpret the call as much more serious trouble than it really was. "Plus, detention seemed to be working," I said to the administrator. Michael nodded that that was true.

"It is policy that you call both parents every time you assign detention," the administrator said, and huffed out of the room to prepare a report to the principal and copy to me. I knew that teachers were supposed to call parents for everything from missing homework assignments to behavior bordering on felonious, but I didn't know that it was a strict written policy that detention required a call. Plus, I'd spent so much time trying to reach the parents, grandmothers, sisters, aunts, or whoever of so many truly troubled and troublesome students with so little success that calling Michael's parents seemed fruitless.

Time was a major issue at Latinate, both for the other teachers and for myself. I spent virtually every waking hour—5 a.m. to 10 p.m.—all week long on my teacher duties. Lessons, backup lessons, tutoring students during lunch and after school, PowerPoints, grading, inputting data, inputting more data, meeting with parents, observing experienced teachers to learn their techniques, meeting with my bosses, writing mandatory "reflections" on those meetings, updating databases, writing reports, trying to get help from someone—*anyone*—for the struggling or out-of-the-control students in some of my classes, and inputting more data.

After climbing the corporate ladder and having had teenage jobs cleaning ovens and scooping dog poop, I can honestly say that I've never had a worse, more demoralizing, more enervating job than teaching at Latinate Institute. Every second of the day was filled with demands and—sadly—students whose needs still weren't being addressed despite all the efforts I could put in.

Instead, Michael was probably referring to the scoldings I had received once first period started and the ninth grade writing workshop got under way. The assistant principal had told me at the beginning of the school year that Latinate was to be a "cathedral of learning," which meant no kids shouting out answers and no noisy class discussions about topics the kids really cared about, such as fast food, video games, cell phones, or flamboyant, middle-finger-flashing rapper Nicki Minaj. Or, as my immediate boss, the English lead teacher, put it, "Don't get the kids excited."

When I started as an English and writing teacher, I had naïvely thought that my mission *was* to get the kids excited about everything from sentence structure to vocabulary. If that excitement sometimes was boisterous, so what? But almost immediately I was informed that at Latinate, if there was to be any excitement of learning, it had to be channeled silently. I was great at generating enthusiasm and engaging the students—moving around the classroom, pulling answers, opinions, and smart-ass remarks out of them—but with their excitement, there often came noise, and I was having a hell of a time turning down the volume.

Recently, the noise rule had been violated so seriously in my classroom that it seemed inevitable that I would be permanently signing off the Smart Board before the school year was out. The reason? We'd been singing "The Star-Spangled Banner." Singing in English class? Chances are, that had never happened before at Latinate. And to make matters worse, I joined in when Michael, Mark, Pashima, and the others spontaneously erupted into song.

Here's the quick backstory: Just the previous evening, Christina Aguilera had famously botched our national anthem at the Super Bowl. To engage my students in the class (song lyrics are poetry, after all), I asked them if they would fare any better and scheduled a quiz for the next day that would determine their knowledge of the lyrics. But before I could finish making the assignment, the kids started singing.

Almon, an A-average boy whose parents had emigrated from the Dominican Republic by way of Milwaukee, Wisconsin, was absolutely sure our national anthem includes the lyric "cheese bursting in air."

Daria, who came from Honduras just a few years ago and was struggling with English, was gamely singing, trying to guess what words would be appropriate for a song about her new country. "Nice!" "Nice! In air!"

While Sarah, the daughter of Ghanaian immigrants, got every word right, and hit every note—even the impossibly high ones—with church-choir perfection. And from Rikkie—the highly intelligent, perhaps brilliant boy whose father was serving six years in an upstate prison—to Cristofer, a skinny kid who fancied himself a Puerto Rican tough, to A'Don, whose mother didn't speak English, to Michael, whose mother *and* father didn't speak English, to Macon, who only seemed to care about basketball, we sang loud, we sang laughing, we sang whatever words we knew and we sang for all we were worth.

Considering that there's no daily Pledge of Allegiance in New York City Public Schools, and that American flags are almost as scarce, they did quite well.

"The dawn's early light" hadn't echoed off the linoleum floor before an administrator and the school aide were in the doorway ready to quell this "disruption," as they did with so many of my classes. But when they realized what we were singing, they backed out, as though they didn't want to be accused of quashing patriotism.

This high-spirited, everybody-participates approach made the ninth grade writing workshop a joy for me. And, as I saw, for my students.

If I assigned a list of spelling words or read a short story in class, I needed all of my energy and wits as a teacher to keep the texting, talking, sleeping, and wrestling matches in check. But make it an eighty-word assignment on "Would you give up your cell phone for one year for $500?" and almost every student—even those who never did any other schoolwork—handed in a paper. When I read these essays to the class in dramatic, radio-announcer fashion, there was silence punctuated by hoots of laughter or roars of agreement or disagreement.

Within days of stepping into the classroom, I realized that I wasn't going to make much progress with these kids by trying to be a stern taskmaster, as I'd been instructed to do by the principal and assistant principal. A year of graduate-school teacher training, as well as my ongoing grad-school coursework, stressed the idea of *getting* the kids to pay attention and do the work, not *forcing* them to pay attention and do the work. And at Latinate, I quickly discovered that by amping up the typical middle-school and high school theme with offbeat questions and high-energy antics, I could get almost everybody writing and involved in the class. In other words, they were actively *learning*.

The eighty-word essay was our daily warm-up and main attraction:

"The best video gaming system is _____."

"If I could live anywhere in the world, I would live in _____."

"My favorite food is _____."

"The grossest thing I ever saw was _____."

"The stupidest thing I've ever done was _____."

"Flying saucers: Real or not?"

"I love—or hate—snow."

"The worst pet in the world would be _____."

It was almost magic. It was really fun. And with that as the intro, we moved into the main lesson—writing narratives and essays—though I often could squeeze in some information on spelling, even punctuation. Five months into the school year, the self-consciousness that often freezes young writers was finally disappearing. In addition to the daily eighty-word exercises, the students had already produced an impressive body of work, including personal narratives, fictional stories with protagonists and antagonists, and five-paragraph essays that supported specific claims.

Many were using periods and commas quite fluently. And everybody had finally gotten the message that "Its" only gets an apostrophe when it's a contraction for "It is." But, as the singing proved, their enthusiasm couldn't always be contained. And that, by itself, seemed to prove to the administration that I was anything but a good teacher.

So I was leaving. I had dropped a letter on the principal's secretary's desk two weeks before, telling her I was resigning but asking for two weeks more with my students. I was returning to publishing, where I had spent the previous twenty-plus years as a writer, editor, and senior editorial executive for one of the world's largest magazine publishers. I had come to this school in the South Bronx with good intentions and the hope of "making a difference." I had voluntarily traded an office in a Manhattan skyscraper for first-year-teacher pay and a swelteringly hot classroom on the third floor of a former elementary school that shared the street with a hospital and a jail.

I want to make it clear that I didn't have the audacity to think that I could just move from the corporation straight to the classroom and succeed. Between the two careers, I'd spent a year in graduate school studying to be a teacher. I enrolled in Empire State College (ESC), a division of the State University of New York. ESC's three-year master's of teaching program used online, in-person, and in-the-classroom training alongside veteran teachers to make career-changers like me provisionally licensed and ready to be hired upon completion of the first year. I finished the first year, and then, while I taught at Latinate, continued to take classes toward the degree, with my coursework bringing ESC professors to my school to watch me in action.

It was a significant investment of time and money. But I believed that teachers were needed in places not far from the comfortable Long Island home I share with my wife, Demetria, and our teenage daughter, Aidan, who attends a well-funded suburban public school. I had read—or perhaps more accurately, I had gotten the impression—that schools in the poorer parts of New York City were desperate for teachers. There were ads on the subway encouraging career-changers to make a difference by joining the NYC Teaching Fellows. The national press was awash in good feelings about the Teach for America program.

I had taken to heart the notion that America was involved in a tug of war between educating the next generation and losing them to illiteracy. I wanted to help out, to make a difference, and I felt that I was in a position, financially and psychologically, to join in pulling the rope for the side of learning and to help these kids. So I set to work getting the training to do so.

Yet, somehow, even with this training and a lot of hands-on preparatory experience, I'd still quickly joined the ranks of the bad teachers we always read about. So aside from me, who were all of these bad teachers?

Was it Ms. Patel, the scholarly English teacher who was assigned to Latinate after the large South Bronx high school in which she had taught for twenty-four and a half years was officially "closed," only to be reopened as several smaller high schools in the same building with new staffs?

In the classroom, Ms. Patel was serious, demanding, and very knowledgeable. She had spent so much of her career in the South

Bronx that she knew how to deal with the language and social problems that many of the kids face. What she couldn't handle to the principal's satisfaction was discipline.

"I have never seen anything like this," Ms. Patel told me. "There is nothing you can do with those students who don't want to learn."

She pointed out that in her previous school—as in many old-line schools—when a student became too disruptive, the teacher went to the door and summoned an assistant principal who removed the disruptive kid from class. Latinate's principal, Ms. P, however, was vehemently against this long-used approach. It offended her view of Latinate as a cathedral of learning. If the teacher couldn't engage a student to want to learn or at least be quiet, the teacher was clearly a failure. To make sure Ms. Patel's teaching was reviewed in the worst possible light, the assistant principal performed an official observation the day before Thanksgiving.

It's common knowledge among teachers everywhere that kids are especially distracted and unruly the day before a break. They expect to goof off, share Skittles and Jolly Ranchers, and perhaps watch a movie. Years of schooling have taught students that teachers indulge them the day before a holiday. But at Latinate, Ms. P insisted, "every day is a full day of instruction." Needless to say, with a riotous, uncooperative class, Ms. Patel received an Unsatisfactory for her pedagogy.

"I don't believe it!" she said one day in exasperation, the lilt of her native India in her voice. "After all of these years of exemplary reviews—exemplary! I have never gotten anything less than an exemplary review from a principal—I come here and get a U."

Today, "exemplary" isn't an official rating in the New York City system. The best a teacher can hope for these days is "Satisfactory." "Unsatisfactory" and "Doubtful" (reserved just for beginning teachers) are the only other authorized ratings. And despite what we read in the press about the powerful teachers' union providing ironclad protection for the incompetent, lazy, and nutty, each school's principal has a great deal of power in the form of a U—Unsatisfactory—rating.

As the city's Department of Education (DOE) publication "Rating Pedagogical Staff Members" makes clear, much more than classroom performance is considered:

> In arriving at the rating, all events, incidents, and staff development activities which occurred during the rating period should be taken into account. The criteria to be used for the evaluation should include personal and professional growth, pupil guidance and instruction, classroom management, participation in school and community activities, and attendance and lateness.

With such a large canvas on which to paint a teacher's performance, the principal has quite a free hand in dispensing an Unsatisfactory. And for a New York City teacher, a U is very bad, indeed. As the DOE's rating guide points out:

> Receipt of an Unsatisfactory rating has serious implications. Unsatisfactory performance is a compelling reason for recommending the Discontinuance of Probationary Service or the Denial of Certification of Completion of Probation and for filing charges against tenured employees. It may also impact an employee's ability to obtain additional licenses.
>
> Employees who have not reached their maximum salary also suffer the loss of annual salary increases.

In other words, a new teacher who ends the school year with a U is out of the city system. I had a preliminary U rating early in the year, and each day, a final, fatal U became more likely. That would mean I could no longer teach in New York City. But at least I had other career options to turn to, including my old profession in publishing. To a veteran, tenured teacher like Ms. Patel, a U meant her salary would be stalled and the chances of going to another school where she could make more of a difference would be nil. Essentially, her career would be over.

No wonder Ms. Patel saw her U as a slap in the face. In fact, it was most likely a bullying invitation to retire. As Ms. Lyons, a veteran science teacher who took me under her wing, was always quick to point out: a principal could hire two brand-new, disposable teachers for what one experienced, highly educated teacher (like herself or Ms. Patel) costs.

"Like any business, these schools have a budget," Ms. Lyons said. "And cutting teacher salaries…"

"…goes right to the bottom line," I said, finishing her sentence.

Was Mr. Bookbinder a bad teacher? His latest rating—U—indicated so. As a veteran teacher, Mr. Bookbinder, too, suffered from being high on the pay scale, and as a former professional actor, he often shared his enthusiasm for the material and broke the rule about not getting the kids "excited." He was well liked by his students, and despite working with the eleventh graders on college applications and undergraduate preparedness, he wasn't considered devoted enough to Ms. P.

But clearly, this bad teacher phenomenon wasn't confined to Latinate Institute. I received hundreds of "Thank you" and "So true!" comments when I published the aforementioned essay about my experience at Latinate on Salon.com.

"Right on target! That's my life! Just the tip of the iceberg!"

commiserating teachers said. So many teachers spoke up about this that it seemed hard to believe so many of our educators could be that *bad*. So there must have been another issue at hand.

———

As my kids filled the classroom on my last day as a teacher, Edgar, a Dominican kid who loved baseball, high-top fade haircuts, and fancy sunglasses ("Edgar! You're out of uniform!" was a typical refrain from me each day) brought in a bakery cake. Opening the white box, I saw "Thank you, Mr. Owens" inscribed in icing. Suddenly, they confirmed what I had suspected. Despite their constant efforts to outmaneuver me with talking, cell-phone-checking, and sharing answers on everything from homework to quizzes, many of the students appreciated me as much as I appreciated the chance to work with them.

Then there were the construction-paper cards from them that made fun of my efforts to learn their slang ("We O.D. dumb tight gonna miss you"), thanked me for helping them ("I learned a lot about writing with more feeling and emotions"), and asked me to stay ("Please, Mr. Owens, don't go! You gonna make me cry!").

The girls hugged me. The boys shook my hand. Cristofer, the tough guy whose father had died, thanked me for teaching him to tie his tie. Rikkie, whose father was serving six years upstate, still hadn't mastered that skill, despite my many attempts to teach him and his obvious intelligence, and begged me to help him once more. As I knotted the plaid fabric, I almost burst into tears.

Good teacher? Bad teacher? I suppose it's how you measure it.

According to "official data," Latinate was hardly one of the worst public schools in New York City. Each year, the city's Department of Education grades the schools' performance—based on "student progress toward graduation, performance on standardized tests and coursework, and student attendance, as well as surveys of parents, students, and teachers about their schools"— and gives them a letter grade from A down to F. The year I was at Latinate, it received a B.* So my school was supposedly better than many—and I couldn't stay.

Some sources estimate that 50 percent of the teachers currently in classrooms across America will either retire or leave the profession over the next five to seven years. The National Commission on Teaching and America's Future (NCTAF) has studied the issue, and in a 2007 report said its findings "are a clear indication that America's teacher dropout problem is spiraling out of control." Further:

> Teacher attrition has grown by 50 percent over the past 15 years. The national teacher turnover rate has risen to 16.8 percent. In urban schools it is over 20 percent, and, in some schools and districts, the teacher dropout rate is actually higher than the student dropout rate. By allowing excessive teacher turnover to continue unabated year after year, we have been digging a deep hole for ourselves.

Until we recognize that we have a retention problem, we will continue to engage in a costly annual recruitment and hiring cycle,

---

*In 2011, 32.7 percent (128 schools) of New York City's 495 high schools received an A; 31.6 percent (124 schools) received a B; 24.0 percent (94 schools) received a C; 8.2 percent (32 schools) received a D; and 3.6 percent (14 schools) received an F, according to the city Department of Education's annual "Progress Report." There is no way to compare these grades with schools elsewhere, since New York City, like most jurisdictions, uses its own proprietary system.

pouring more and more teachers into our nation's classrooms only to lose them at a faster and faster rate. This will continue to drain our public tax dollars. It will undermine teaching quality, and it will most certainly hinder our ability to close student achievement gaps.

Nationwide, high teacher turnover in high-needs schools is the result of the school environments, not the teachers' lack of interest in working with the students. A 2011 report by Jason A. Grissom and Lael Keiser of the University of Missouri showed that teacher turnover was not correlated with school poverty, but with principal effectiveness. As a principal's effectiveness rating rose, the probability of a teacher's leaving significantly dropped.

Everyone needs to understand that teacher turnover happens at a very high cost to the kids. Nationwide, an increasing number of children at all income levels face unstable home lives. A 2012 report in *Pediatrics in Review*, a publication of the American Academy of Pediatrics, said that 50 percent of all first marriages will end in divorce, affecting more than one million children each year. The Centers for Disease Control and Prevention's "Morbidity and Mortality Weekly Report" in December 2010 cited a 2009 study showing that 26.6 percent of adults over eighteen years old reported experiencing parental divorce or separation during their own childhood. For children in a high-needs school such as Latinate, that number is even higher, and the instability of their family lives is ongoing. Many live in broken, single-mother homes or move from relative to relative on a regular basis. One of my eighth graders lived with his mother in a series of homeless shelters and would only show up when they were in a shelter near the school.

That their teachers are not a stable presence in their lives is quite sad. School should provide a model of stability, but with the way teachers are churned through the system these days, the authority figure of the teacher tends to be as evanescent as many other adults in these students' lives.

On my last day, the ninth-grade girl Pashima teared up and, looking into my eyes, asked, "You going away and ain't never coming back?" My heart stung as I realized this probably wasn't the first or last time she would utter those words.

Voices of Teachers around the Country

James Boutin, Language Arts and Social Studies Teacher, Seattle, Washington

For quite some time now, the American public has been told over and over again by movies, romances, newspapers, and politicians that the best teachers are miracle workers. We've been led to believe that great teachers (and in many cases, great teachers alone) have the capacity to take any group of low-performing students and raise their academic achievement to heights on par with any student in the country, or at least reach them in a way nobody else could.

After all, Jaime Escalante did it in *Stand and Deliver*. Erin Gruwell did it in *Freedom Writers*. And LouAnne Johnson did it in *Dangerous Minds* (with the super-touching tagline: "She broke the rules...and changed their lives").

Additionally, William Taylor, a young math teacher in Washington, D.C., who was featured in *Waiting for "Superman,"* brought a classroom with 40 percent of the students scoring on grade level to a place where 90 percent of them were scoring on grade level. When Michelle Rhee, the former chancellor of District of Columbia Public Schools and now a famous "reformer," was a teacher, her students "went from the 13th percentile in standardized national tests to the 90th percentile." In only one year, the 2005 National Teacher of the Year, Jason Kamras, managed to drop the percentage of his students scoring below basic from 80 percent to 40 percent.

All of these movies, articles, romances, and sound bites feed into a larger national narrative with a plot line that goes something like this: There are a bunch of poor, uneducated kids in this country because the schools have failed them with awful teachers (problem). Luckily, there are a bunch of idealistic, capable young people who are willing to give a few years of their lives to help them and save public education (solution). The kids can be saved by teachers alone (conclusion).

Policy-makers, superintendents, and professional-development gurus make a lot of these teachers' stories. Over and over again, I've heard these "reformers" say things like, "You don't have to change a student's socio-economic status, their home life, or their history. All you have to do is put a great teacher in front of them and they will succeed." And this really isn't an argument you want to find yourself on the other side of. If you disagree and argue that a student's home life does matter, you're easily dismissed as someone who doesn't really believe in children. And who wants to be tagged that way in the middle of a debate?

"You don't think their academic abilities can be raised

without changing their home lives? Then you must be a racist or bigot. How dare you assume they're not capable! You must not be a very good teacher, or else you would have made great progress with them."

"But, uh, I can never reach their parents. I can never get them to stay after school. I can never get them to attend Saturday school. What else am I supposed to do?"

"Well, if you were a better teacher, they'd want to come. Maybe you should find a new line of work."

And the argument is over, and it's pretty clear that the any-kid-can-make-great-gains argument is triumphant.

But there are reasons to be wary of this narrative. To begin with, most of the inspirational teacher movies you see, while based on a true story, alter significant realities, which deludes the viewer into a misunderstanding of teaching.

Take Jamie Escalante as an example. *Stand and Deliver* would have you believe that Escalante decided one day that he was going to teach calculus at a low-achieving school. All the rest of the teachers told him he was crazy and apparently hoped he would fail. But he did it, and his students all passed the AP exam. The story implies that you can take any student, no matter what their ability or home situation, and teach them any advanced topic of study, such as calculus. This didn't happen in reality. It took Escalante ten years to reach the success the movie depicts. And he did it by building a strong math program from the ground up, not by taking students struggling with arithmetic in high school and getting them to calculus within a year.

Or take Erin Gruwell in *Freedom Writers*. If the movie

is to be believed, Gruwell had only one class of students for the entire day, and she was allowed to have the same class in the following years. I know of no full-time teacher who's afforded that luxury, especially in our most challenging schools.

Although many future teachers are inspired by these films, I've yet to meet a real teacher in a real school who isn't somewhat offended by the ease with which reaching our most challenged students is portrayed: Just give up your life for the kids and they'll all go to college. Not quite. It's probably not a good sign when real teachers mock the techniques used by movie teachers.

Also, many of the teachers who are publicized for their students' outstanding achievements lack proof for their claims. Michelle Rhee famously has no evidence of her students' rising from the 13th percentile to the 90th. Another interesting reality plaguing many of these educators is that very few of them stay in the classroom longer than a few years. Michelle Rhee stayed for three; William Taylor is in his fourth and recently received his administrative certificate; Erin Gruwell left teaching after seeing her students graduate to work at the collegiate level; and Jason Kamras stayed for a whole eight years after beginning with Teach for America.

The "magical teacher" narrative would have us believe that you need very little experience in the classroom to be excellent, but also (if you pay attention to the details) that our best teachers don't really enjoy teaching enough to stick with it. (Sadly, research seems to bear this out.) But perhaps that's because their success on paper belies their experience. Or maybe because they always had other ambitions in life beyond just teaching—but I wouldn't want to draw any conclusions. It does strike me as odd, though, that the teachers who write and star in all the inspirational movies, books, and articles about their amazing success are no longer actually teaching.

James Boutin teaches language arts and social studies at a small school near Seattle. He previously taught in New York City; Washington, D.C.; Renton, Washington; and Knoxville, Tennessee. He blogs at www.anurbanteachers education.com.

THE ALMIGHTY PRINCIPAL

The single most important characteristic of a good school is a strong principal. It may seem obvious, but this simple fact is too often overlooked: The principal is the most important person in the building. A good principal can turn a school around against daunting odds…. A bad principal can, just as surely, demoralize a staff, squander money, and alienate parents. As the late Ronald Edmonds wrote: "There are no good schools with bad principals."

—Clara Hemphill, "Public Schools That Work" in *City Schools,* 2000

R UN AWAY!" THE LITTLE man gushed, crouching next to me to hide behind the counter separating the main office from the waiting area. "Really, run away! The principal will give you a U. She gives everybody a U!"

His eyes bugging, his breath hot on my face, he could tell I thought he was crazy.

"Really!" he pleaded. "I've been in the System for twenty-two years, and I've never seen anything like it! The way she treats teachers is terrible. Terrible!"

Everyone involved with the New York City Department of Education calls it the System. I found out later that just days before, this science teacher and long-term survivor of the System had been punched in the face by a summer-school student. Nonetheless, the most important message he had was about the beating I might get from the principal.

I'd read about the school's tyrannical principal on the Internet, but c'mon! How bad could she be? I'm a veteran of major corporations. In my career I've been through buyouts, upheavals, management shake-ups, and every manner of cruelty and weirdness known to desk jockeys. I smiled politely at the guy, and he got the message that I wasn't going to run. I was staying for my interview at Latinate Institute.

Started six years earlier on the third floor of a former elementary school, Latinate is a 350-student "institute" "designed to promote academic excellence that directly leads to college entrance and success." Another totally separate, slighter larger, and widely praised small high school occupies the first two floors of the building. In addition to the hospital up the block on one side and the jail down the block on the other side, Latinate is surrounded by churches, *iglesias*, tabernacles, assemblies, and Gospel temples of various sizes and denominations. Chickens make their home in rundown houses and overgrown lots that dot the street, frequently pecking away on the sidewalk outside the school, and roosters crow loudly all day long, giving a rural soundtrack to a decidedly urban neighborhood that sits in the shadow of towering apartment buildings.

Founded on the noble mission of helping kids who otherwise wouldn't go to college, Latinate, like an increasing number of public schools, received start-up funding from several foundations and educational organizations, in addition to government funds. When I arrived, Latinate boasted a "100 percent college-acceptance rate." I wasn't quite convinced, since many excellent schools don't achieve that, but I initially didn't question it.

Before my interview, I stumbled on some comments about Latinate on the Internet:

"HELL is the only way to describe Latinate," a self-described student posted on InsideSchools.org. "This school has given me nightmares and it'll give you some, too."

"The students are out of control," said a parent.

"There is no consistent discipline and the principal is overwhelmed," wrote one teacher.

Still, I wasn't put off by any of these remarks. Comments like these aren't uncommon about any school. Especially those in New York City. Hundreds of high schools and middle schools get the same treatment, especially at the hands of anonymous posters like these. Plus, reading the comments about Latinate from 2007 and 2008, I figured the atmosphere must have changed in a couple of years.

So I ignored the fact that the crazed science teacher and a 2008 posting agreed on one thing—that a job at Latinate is a U-filled experience and a career-ender.

As I sat waiting for my interview, my concern wasn't getting fired but getting hired. The Department of Education's annual hiring freeze had just been lifted, and here I was, thrilled at the prospect of helping underprivileged kids and waiting for my interview. And waiting. And waiting.

Three hours later, I was ushered into a classroom to provide a demonstration of my teaching.

Imagine you have to run away and go into hiding. You don't know how long you'll be away. Food is taken care of. And you can bring only what will fit into a backpack. What do you bring?

So began my sample lesson on Anne Frank's *The Diary of a*

Young Girl, a staple of eighth-grade English. My audience was a dozen eleventh-grade summer-school students, a couple of teachers, and an assistant principal.

"I'd take my cell phone," said one boy, tapping the pocket where his BlackBerry peeked out.

"Good," I told him. "But you're going into hiding. And if you use your phone they'll be able to track you."

"I'd bring a flashlight and a rope," said another.

"I'd bring a computer."

"I'd bring Pringles."

"Food is taken care of," I reminded him.

"I'd still bring Pringles."

"I'd bring an Xbox."

"I'd bring my eye makeup."

And so it went as I introduced the book. One girl toward the front picked up all of the cues and ran with them.

"The family was going to be sent to a death camp, so they hid out in the back of a building for years," she said, raising her eyes to the ceiling as she spoke, as though she was reciting the most obvious information.

"You're smart," said a boy toward the back.

"We read this book in eighth grade," she said.

Apparently nobody else had, but the students stuck with me as I introduced them to the Nazis, the Holocaust, and the Second World War. Several had no idea who the Nazis were, what the Holocaust was, or even what century I was talking about. But they enjoyed evading direct answers to my questions and watching me try to bring them back to the topic when they made fun of my bald spot. It was school as usual until I told them that the Frank family couldn't flush the toilet during the day. And the lesson really hit home when I briefly wouldn't let any of them leave the room to pee as an example of what they had to go through.

"But I've got to pee," said one.

"Me, too," said another.

"Yeah, I got to go," moaned a third.

"Well, hold it," I said sternly. "You can't leave. Just like Anne Frank couldn't leave."

That cinched it. The look on the assistant principal's face told me I had the job. The following day I was hired as an English teacher at Latinate.

"I assume you know your subject matter," said Latinate's assistant principal for curriculum, who didn't even ask me what I knew about English literature. "At our school, classroom management is very, very important. And you did well with that."

A chubby man in his early sixties who was fond of dying his hair black, the assistant principal told me how he "loved to read a great novel and discuss the meaning of life." He smiled, sighed wistfully, and then turned suddenly serious. "But we can't do that at our school. We have to focus on basic skills and class-room management."

If the students I had just met were any indication of what lay ahead, I was eager for it. They were Hispanic, African-American, and African immigrant kids who didn't seem hostile to learning, just bored. And I, like every new teacher, thought that all I needed was energy blended with lessons that showed how life and literature were related. *They'd be inspired; they'd hunger for knowledge; they'd work hard at their studies; they'd succeed....* I signed on for $45,530 a year.

"I hope you will do a good job," the assistant principal said flatly as I eagerly accepted the job. "If you need help, we will hire a coach for you."

His lukewarm encouragement was slightly worrisome. In the past, whenever I had been hired for a job—or in the dozens of instances where I'd hired people—there always was a big smile, optimistic words, and a positive, "can-do" spirit. Yet I sensed that the assistant principal's tepid words weren't aimed exclusively at me. He barely knew me. Most people spend more time getting to know their waiters at TGI Friday's than he had spent going over my qualifications.

Clearly, the finer points of academic preparation and life experience weren't an issue. Rather, what counted was meeting some still-undefined standard of performance that included "basic skills and classroom management." I felt a caution light of foreboding illuminate inside me as I realized that whatever this standard was, it would not be easily met. After all, he clearly had been through this drill many times before and knew better than to be too positive.

Plus, despite my enthusiasm for the kids, the little science teacher's words kept ringing in my ears. "Run away! The principal will give you a U! She gives everyone a U!" So I was anticipating my first encounter with her with more than a little dread.

Meeting Ms. P came soon after. A three-day new-teacher orientation held at the school immediately after I was hired was a bizarre boot camp/educational philosophy seminar/brainwashing session/summer camp with a hyperactive copying machine. All under the strict direction of Ms. P, the founding principal of Latinate Institute. Not merely "principal," but "founding principal." And always "Ms. P."

"She would take a bullet for her school," the assistant principal told me. "Take a bullet."

A large, round woman in her late thirties, Ms. P kept her hair pulled back tightly. Her eyebrows were long, thin, and very expressive, moving up and down like a caffeinated drawbridge. Ms. P's large mouth was in a constant state of frowning disapproval or condescending fake hilarity. I didn't feel especially comfortable around her. She spoke of a collegial atmosphere, but it quickly became apparent that she saw herself as an imperial figure who "shared" her ideas with her "staff." I got the sense that she looked at us as "the help," whose job was to execute her instructions with the silent efficiency of a hotel bellman who's told, "Take these bags to Room 328."

That half of the staff had turned over at this tiny school since June—eight new teachers, a new dean, and a new administrator—should have been orientation enough for me. Historically, a typical New York City school would see one out of eight teachers leave each year. But as school reform and tight budgets have taken hold, teacher turnover has soared. Under the cover of booting bad teachers, expensive, experienced teachers are pushed out and replaced by beginners who, as my friend Ms. Lyons pointed out, cost less than half as much. At Latinate, the staff turnover was close to 50 percent a year.

As we underwent orientation, the assistant principal kept bringing in more new teachers.

"This is Ms. Sanchez, the new Spanish teacher…."

An hour later, "This is Mr. Steinman, the new social studies teacher…."

The next morning, "This is," the assistant principal paused, looking down at the paper in his hand, "Ms. Raphael, another new Spanish teacher…."

And so it went until the new-staff meetings segued into a full-staff weekend retreat at a plush hotel-conference center in a leafy New Jersey suburb. While most of Latinate's students live in the grimmest part of New York, we were provided Garden State rooms and restaurant meals. I don't know whether New York City's taxpayers footed the bill or the money came from some hedge-fund-financed "staff development" account, but it seemed odd that we were in New Jersey when our students were in New York. Regardless of the geography, Ms. P made sure we earned every bite and thread-count. As with the three days spent at school, the schedule was a merciless parade of presentations, discussions, handouts, and team-building exercises that had us on our feet every few hours.

We played Simon Says, while Ms. P looked on, laughing. She wanted us to believe she was providing good-natured encouragement, but I noticed that she never took part in activities that made the participants look foolish. That was reserved for teachers. We had to find something we had in common with another teacher ("You like soft brownies?! Me, too!"), or share a secret ("I have two fake teeth." "When I was a boy, I wanted to be a nun. They smelled so good"), or join sweaty hands and turn human chains into knots, while Ms. P looked on, laughing.

Ms. P lectured on the institute's mission statement. ("Our mission is to develop high-achieving students of good character who use academic, technological, and social skills to inspire others, succeed in college, and accede to positions of social power that advance their community and the broader nation.") She also explained the institute's vision statement and quizzed us on the difference between that and the mission statement. ("The mission statement is our here and now." "The vision statement is where I see us going.")

If the mission statement was ambitious, the vision statement was an 800-word manifesto that made the island paradise in Thomas More's *Utopia* seem second best to Ms. P's Latinate. It was to be a place that develops "the whole child—academically, socially, and emotionally" and is a showcase of "exemplary teaching practices," featuring "a personalized program with academic interventions that meet every student's individual needs." Not only will teachers have "the time, support, and resources necessary," but the Institute also "will form strategic partnerships and working relationships with other schools, community-based organizations, universities, and businesses to initiate and maintain the sharing of best practices, comprehensive after-school offerings, and other resources." By the time Ms. P and her staff were finished, the institute's graduates would have "the skills and character to lead and motivate others and succeed in college, their careers, and life!"

This language of great expectations was contained in promotional material for the school that had been prepared when Latinate first opened six years before. Much at the school had changed in that time, but the brochure was still in use. With full-color photographs and zippy design, it showcased an institute with high hopes as well as:

- An accelerated college-preparatory curriculum.
- Peer mentoring.
- Academic tutoring and homework help.
- A technology program.
- An ethics/service learning seminar.
- An art history program.
- A comprehensive after-school program with chess, step/hip-hop and ballroom dancing, basketball, tennis, fencing, film-making, and chorus.

By the time I got to Latinate, the only things I could find from this list that still existed were basketball and Ms. P's high hopes.

Unable to actually deliver what had been called "special school features," Ms. P poured the pressure on the teachers. My notebook from the orientation and retreat is dense with teacher "musts."

- We must provide the children with rich, purposeful lessons.
- We must support the social, emotional, and academic needs of all students.
- We must conduct weekly advisory meetings during a non-teaching period and give the children a safe environment and safe haven where they can set goals, ask questions, and build self-esteem in an empathetic, nonjudgmental environment.
- We must devote one period a day to professional service, with Ms. P assigning us to duties such as monitoring the cafeteria or critiquing the performance of other teachers as they moderate their advisory groups.
- We must ensure that every failing mark for each marking period is reversed to a passing mark via makeup work (such as independent study or packets) for the students in our advisory groups.
- We must help students who fail nonetheless recover credit for their failed courses.
- We must organize a celebratory event for our advisory groups at least once per semester (field trip, dinner, bowling, a movie, or other activity).
- We must guide our students through at least two community service projects a year.
- We must never count on the copier working.

Throughout the weekend, there were PowerPoint presentations on New York State standards, curriculum maps, lesson plans, syllabi, baseline data, acuity tests, Regents exams, S.M.A.R.T.

goals, and the Blackboard Configuration (the only way Ms. P permitted teachers to set up a lesson). Hour after hour, each topic was presented as "the most important thing we will cover during this retreat."

Then, of course, there was a team-building exercise. ("I'm John, and I like to fish." "I'm Regina, and I like coffee.") Who could argue with this? The concept appeared to be great lessons, strong teachers, involved students, and a collegial atmosphere...

But at the weekend retreat in New Jersey, late on Sunday afternoon, I suddenly was overcome by a wave of panic. Every muscle tightened, and I was consumed by a fight-or-flight reflex born of adrenaline rushing through my body. It was instantaneous, unexpected, and overwhelming. My unconscious mind was shouting to me as desperately as that little science teacher who had implored me to "Run away! Really, run away!"

At that moment I knew precisely what I was facing: Ms. P was not just an imperial figure; she had a serious case of Crazy Boss syndrome. As someone who has been a boss and been subject to all manner of bosses, I know the problem well. Ms. P was demanding—that's fine. But she was delusional about what could be absorbed and achieved.

What triggered my panic attack was that, after all the handouts, PowerPoints, and relentless, notebook-filling rules, rubrics, standards, demands, and musts, Ms. P gave us several website URLs and sent us to a row of computers at the conference hotel with orders to immediately integrate this knowledge into our instructional practice. We were to spend a half-hour applying various state standards to our curriculum maps and ensuring that the lessons were rigorous enough to make the students "college ready, not just college eligible." Like my weary colleagues, I dragged myself to a computer, numb in the realization that Ms. P was oblivious to how drained everyone was, and that only so much can be jammed into a weekend retreat.

Therein lay the problem. As a Crazy Boss, Ms. P didn't see limits in what people can physically do. Despite her own failure to achieve the grand plans for everything from a technology program to after-school fencing and ballroom dancing, Ms. P had the notion that her teachers could and would do everything she thought up. And it would be done perfectly. Ms. P had so many "Amazing!" ideas, programs, and initiatives that a mere mortal teacher could never keep up. For all the lip service about helping kids, she really was all about jargon, process, and spreadsheets. What she had sent us to the computers to do was just digital paperwork. It wasn't really useful instructional material. Just fodder for data.

And I realized that whatever facets of education Ms. P couldn't express as data she would express as a *show*. It was all about creating a school that was really a show, a pageant that made it *look* like these high school students—many of whom I would come to realize had few, if any, of the most basic academic skills—were "scholars." (She often used that word to describe the kids.) Looking back, even I could have seen that turning Latinate into a silent, reverent cathedral of learning wasn't about to happen any time soon with kids who had been in school for more than a decade and hadn't gotten the message yet that their job was to sit down and be quiet.

She was the type of boss who believes that the hard part of great ideas is coming up with them. Implementing these great ideas is simply a matter of telling your people to implement them. The results will follow. If the results don't follow, it is because the people were not good at implementing, not because they didn't have any direction or support to do so. In this case, that means they were bad teachers.

Ms. P threw her great ideas at us the way Mardi Gras revelers toss beads in New Orleans. After three days of orientation at the school and two days at the New Jersey retreat, I had amassed hundreds of pages of copies and printouts that supplemented the dozens of topics we'd covered—from how to produce a curriculum map to state standards to setting goals to planning our advisory to the essential components of differentiated instruction to destinations for field trips (Radio City Christmas Spectacular! Madame Tussauds! Maryland!). I was on or referred to more than a dozen websites. I had two thumb drives full of PDFs of lesson plans and state standards. There also were numerous pamphlets and books on advisory and state standards. Not the textbooks we would be using in class—in fact, there had been no discussion about what we would specifically cover in class—instead, this was all material on how to do things the Latinate way. And with each page, each file, and each presentation, it was clear that "*this* is the most important thing in keeping you from receiving a U."

There wasn't an aspect of Latinate life that Ms. P didn't have covered with a demand, edict, or what she called an "expectation." From what I could see, what she practiced wasn't so much management, or even micromanagement, as bizarre stagecraft with moment-by-moment choreography of our day. Her instructions ranged from the simple (stand outside the classroom during the change of classes) to the rococo (a three-page, tightly spaced brief on classroom décor and arrangement, which seemed a little overzealous for teachers who were constantly shifting classrooms throughout the day). I was having a tough time figuring out how I was going to maintain learning stations for scholars with various learning styles—visual, auditory, and kinesthetic—in classrooms that were given hard use (if not trashed) each day in the usual course of business.

For students, there were many, many rules, including zero tolerance for being out of uniform. Or using obscenity (a rule, which enforced, would have given many of my students little to say). The zero-tolerance policy also extended to teachers. We were *required* to learn each student's name; commit to growing professionally; assign homework daily; not eat or drink in front of students except if drinking water and during lunch; not wear jeans, sweats, sneakers, excessive jewelry, low-cut blouses, shorts, mini-skirts, spaghetti straps, or tank tops; and be on time.

Ms. P also required that we teachers keep our young scholars on script by employing a new system called PBIS—Positive Behavioral Interventions and Supports. She insisted we would beat inappropriate behavior by stressing the positive. "Frame everything in a positive way," we were told. "Don't say, 'Don't.'" If a student is running in the hall, don't say, "Don't run." Say, "Please walk." We also learned how to resolve conflicts by using "I statements" rather than "You statements." ("I need you to sit down" is far better than saying, "You and Natasha should stop fighting.") My head was spinning before I stepped into the classroom.

Of course, not every principal is like Ms. P. I met one who seemed quite the opposite.

Shortly before school started—while I waited for the Department of Education to lift its hiring freeze—I visited schools throughout the Bronx. In my job hunt, I was confident that the freeze would be lifted, and when that happened, I would be fresh in each principal's memory.

Mike and Rich, two math teachers who had gone through the same teacher-training program I did at Empire State College a couple of years before, were working together at a Bronx high school. They loved it. And loved their principal. I was eager to meet her and stopped by the school.

A large, modern building that houses several small high schools, it was undergoing construction. The security guards inside the front door couldn't hear a word I said over the roar of cutters and grinders. With a portfolio under my arm, I was waved through. I roamed the dark halls until I came to the High School of Artistic Trades (not its real name), where huge *papier-mâché* sculptures of dragons and tigers hung from the ceiling, and student artwork and college posters covered the walls. With fewer than 400 students, HSAT occupies just a few hallways in the sprawling building.

It's a traditional academic high school, but HSAT, like hundreds of small high schools opened in the city in the last decade, has a theme. There really is the High School for Global Citizenship, the High School of Hospitality Management, the Academy for Conservation and the Environment, the Pablo Neruda Academy for Architecture and World Studies, the Facing History School, as well as dozens more with names incorporating technology, accounting, sports, the arts, and advertising. Some of these schools take their theme seriously and give the students a solid background in the topic. Others have been subsumed in tight budgets, unrealistic expectations, and the daily challenges of keeping test scores and other data up, and now keep the theme alive only in a purposeful name.

"Excuse me," I said, poking my head into the only room in the area that had its light on—an office with the sign "Eileen Scotto, Principal" next to the open door and a small, fortyish woman hunched over papers on her desk. "I'm John Owens, and I'm an English teacher…"

Before I could finish my sentence, I was waved in and sitting at the conference table across from her desk.

"Call me Eileen," she said. "Everybody does. Even the kids."

Over the next half hour, Eileen and I talked about her kids (the ninth through twelfth graders in the school). We talked about her biological children (whose photos decorated her office). We talked about how this school kept cell phones out of the classroom. (Each morning, as the students entered, they stowed their phones in tiny lockers by the door—no exceptions, no excuses.) We talked about Shakespeare. (She started out as an English teacher.) We talked about Mike and Rich. (She loved them.) We talked about my background (writing, reporting). And we talked about our faith in upward mobility and the American Dream.

Tears ran down her cheeks as she described how a former teacher at the school had said that all of these kids shouldn't go to college. "Somebody has to load the trucks," he told her.

"Not these kids," she said defiantly. "We must work with them to get them to college and to succeed in college. We must!"

Her passion, her enthusiasm, and her commitment struck me as very powerful.

"I want to work for you," I said. But as much as I wanted the job, I didn't get it.

Then, within weeks of the start of the school year, the New York media crackled with reports that Eileen was being investigated by the Department of Education for grading practices at the school. According to the *New York Times*, the school had a policy of passing any student who showed up for class regularly and even graduated some who missed many days of school.

I was stunned. In the years before this news broke, outstanding data had propelled HSAT to the top of the DOE's ranking and accountability system. One year, it was rated the best high school in New York City. The school's data was at such a high level that both Eileen and her assistant principal received thousands of dollars in bonuses. When the investigation went public, Eileen was earning $145,493 a year.

"The DOE has absolutely created a climate for these types of scandals to happen," Michael Mulgrew, president of the city's teachers' union told *The Times*. "Their culture of 'measure everything and question nothing a principal tells you' makes it hard to figure out what's real and what's not real inside a school."

The business-bred notion of putting virtually all of the power and scorekeeping in the hands of manager principals has resulted in a wide range of abuses of both the authority and the data. The principal can virtually make up what will be achieved. As in the case of Ms. P and Latinate, kids whose previous academic careers have left them woefully unprepared for middle school or high school would suddenly—thanks to the principal's brilliant ideas executed by her well-choreographed teachers—be college-ready scholars. And if that failed to get the results required, the principal could—as Eileen was accused of doing—fudge the data beyond fiction to the point of perjury.

MEET THE TEACHERS

If I had the ability, which nobody does really, to just design a system and say, "*ex cathedra*, this is what we're going to do," you would cut the number of teachers in half, but you would double the compensation of them, and you would weed out all the bad ones and just have good teachers. And double the class size with a better teacher is a good deal for the students.

—New York City Mayor Michael Bloomberg

A GIRL WITH INFLATABLE falsies goes up in an airplane that isn't pressurized. What happens?"

"Her boobs get really big!"

"Correct. Why?"

"Because there's higher air pressure inside the falsies than in the airplane."

"Correct. And how big will her boobs get?"

"Until the pressure is equal in the boobs and in the airplane… or until the falsies explode!"

Now that was science an eighth grader could love.

Mrs. Valentine, my middle-school science teacher, clearly had a straightforward, matter-of-fact persona that made the subject matter wonderfully exciting, vivid, and unforgettable.

Mr. Venning, my eleventh-grade social studies teacher, regaled us with tales of attending Morehouse College with Martin Luther King, Jr. ("Yeah, but he was so serious. I hung out with his brother, Alfred.")

My teachers were a passionate and inspiring lot, and school had been good to me. Education had opened doors that were locked to my parents and most of those around me in working-class suburbia. I knew firsthand that teachers could be very important and powerful in shaping minds and shaping lives.

I had hard teachers, easy teachers, mean teachers, nice teachers, smart teachers, and clueless teachers, but I never recall having a bad teacher. They had been some of the most influential people in my life. Decades later, I occasionally find myself quoting them.

"Zut alors!" as Miss Waldhutter would say, having worked tirelessly—though futilely—to impress her ninth graders with the beauty of French and modern dance.

Just as I was lucky to have had wonderful teachers when I was in school, I lucked into having a terrific, experienced teacher at Latinate who gave me real-world advice. We met when we happened to sit next to each other during Ms. P's five days of new-teacher orientation. While Ms. P and her "cabinet" tortured us with PowerPoints and explored the issue of young scholars maintaining silence in the cathedral of learning, Ms. Lyons cut to the chase.

"I just give the kids the same look that a state trooper gives when he pulls you over for speeding," she whispered to me. "It's the look that says, 'Something here smells really bad.'"

A short, spirited woman who looked like a younger Whoopi Goldberg, Ms. Lyons had spent eight years teaching science at schools around northern Manhattan and the South Bronx. She was new to Latinate. A victim of wholesale "reform" at her previous school, like Ms. Patel, Ms. Lyons was assigned to Latinate by the Department of Education.

"I don't know how I got put into this school," she sighed. "But the Lord must have a plan for me here."

Her daily commute from her home high in the Hudson Valley was more than 150 miles round trip and required almost four hours on the train.

"It's a lot," she said. "But I love the country and the rents are low."

And as the orientation's interminable acronyms and buzzwords flew and ethereal "student-engagement" processes wafted over our heads, Ms. Lyons whispered straight talk and practical advice to me.

- "Stand outside the classroom door, and give them that state-trooper look," she advised. "Say 'You're not coming into *my* classroom until you tuck in your shirt.'"
- "Tell them to take out their notebooks the same way the state trooper says, 'License and registration.'"
- "Whenever the assistant principal shows up, it's bad news."
- "Don't lean against the wall when you're by the classroom door. A roach can crawl up your back."

Even as a rookie, I knew that everything Ms. Lyons said was valuable and tested under fire. From that moment on, I clung to her as my unofficial mentor.

She loved the kids and could see right away that they weren't being served by the school's pageantry. But as a wise survivor of the System, she knew her only option was to play along. With years of experience and far more than a master's degree, Ms. Lyons was toward the top of the pay scale, and she knew that made her a target for the budget-obsessed Ms. P. So if the principal wanted a cathedral of learning, she'd get it, enforced by state-trooper-grimacing practicality. Ms. Lyons' commitment to the kids was obvious. She was quick to understand and address their strengths, weaknesses, and needs. Like the teachers I had when I was a kid, and like the teachers I encountered in my teacher training, she was a dedicated educator and a good person.

That's why I was surprised when at a Latinate staff meeting early in September, the assistant principal told us it was "morally reprehensible" if we did not do everything we could for every student.

As I looked around Latinate, I wondered who, specifically, had to be reminded of their moral obligation to the kids. I didn't know these people well, and some of them I didn't immediately warm up to—or them to me—but I certainly didn't see anyone who had taken this job or gotten involved in teaching simply to slack off. Unlike so many people I had known in publishing, there was not one among my new colleagues who lived to hear the words, "Okay, the bar's open!"

Despite their tough talk and hard-edged humor, these teachers clearly loved kids and would, without a lot of prompting, tell you about their greatest successes and failures with their students over the years. Wasn't inspiring, empowering, really *teaching* these students enough?

The only topic that they discussed nearly as much as the students at Latinate was how to "survive the System." That is, knowing the city's Department of Education bureaucracy and the details of the United Federation of Teachers' contract so well that you could advocate for yourself as a teacher and maneuver all the pitfalls that could trip you up or even land you on the street. For instance, who gets "excessed" if a school's budget is cut? Every survivor knows it's going to be the least senior teacher in the license area that's being downsized.

When I started at Latinate, I was immediately impressed with the English Department lead teacher, the highest ranking member of Ms. P's "cabinet," who made it clear that she was a teacher because she wanted to help the kids—and help them on their level. No one else seemed to have the kind of buddy-buddy relationships with the students that she did.

"Oh, that's so ghetto," she said to an eleventh-grade girl who visited the school during our orientation. The girl laughed about the comment on her brightly colored, high-heeled shoes, and the lead teacher continued, joking, "Well, that's you. You're so ghetto, right?"

That a white teacher would even dare to joke with an African-American student in that way surprised me. So, too, did the way the lead teacher spoke to Ms. P.

"Oh, don't think *you* can talk to Ms. P like that," she said to me in the hallway one day when she turned from our conversation to deliver a sarcastic compliment to the principal. "You can't. Only I can."

A midsized woman in her late thirties, the lead teacher had spiky brown hair and colorful tunics and slacks, as well as bright, chunky jewelry that made her look like what people outside of New York think New York hipsters look like. She also had numerous tattoos that she liked to explain, particularly those that had references to Jane Austen.

"I'm the lead teacher and I am a feminist," is the way she introduced herself to us at the new-teacher orientation.

The lead teacher had been at Latinate since the early days.

Born and educated in the Pacific Northwest, she moved to New York City after college and got a job in the production side of publishing. In a job filled with data, deadlines, and tracking pages, proofs, color, and printing plants, the production editor reigns over an empire that those of us in the editorial department always thought of as a black box and black hole.

Even after decades in the business, many editorial people aren't quite sure what the production people do, but they are thankful that they do it. Outsiders believe that writers and designers are cut the most slack on a magazine. But in my experience, someone who is willing to do the heavy lifting of production and does it well can smile and tell the editors to get lost at will.

The lead teacher brought her detailed-obsessed skill set and sassy personality to teaching. It was an excellent fit at Latinate. The ability to be detail-obsessed and a creative wise-guy at the same time made her good with the kids, good with the data, and sister-caliber close to Ms. P, but it also made her a sarcastic know-it-all when it came to dealing with the rest of us. If Ms. P's modus operandi was "my way or the highway," the lead teacher was the one holding the map.

So, because she was someone I hoped could teach me a lot, I was solicitous and humble with the lead teacher. When she gave me a thumb drive that contained hundreds of PowerPoints for a ninth-grade writing program that had been developed by a man she called "the best teacher I ever knew," my outpouring of thanks was so profuse that she must have thought I was kidding. But my thanks on receiving those lessons were as heartfelt as when the doctor passed me my newborn daughter. I wanted to help these kids and be the best teacher I could possibly be.

I knew that having a stock of well-proven lessons would let me hit the Smart Board running. There would be no need to reinvent so many aspects of ninth-grade English, and though tweaking and tuning the material to suit my students was going to take a good deal of time, I knew that this material would help me be more efficient and effective. Plus, the lesson plans were already outlined in the basic format that Ms. P required, so after editing each one, I could have the plan printed out and displayed on my desk in case an administrator came by for an inspection. "Grateful" only begins to describe my initial feelings toward the lead teacher.

Like the lead teacher, Mr. Bookbinder also was proud of his relationship with the kids.

"A Jew, a Puerto Rican, and a black guy walk into a bar…" was a typical Bookbinder opening line to anything from class to encountering a kid in the hall.

A former actor, Bookbinder, now in his fifties, looked a lot like the old show-biz icon Danny Kaye. His jokes about Jews, blacks, and whites were positioned as a way to bond with the kids. His girlfriend, with whom he lived just north of the city, was, after all, black.

He had been teaching in the Bronx for eight years and had spent the last four at Latinate. When I arrived, he and the lead teacher were the only survivors in the English Department. Bookbinder and his shtick were likeable and well liked by the kids. He wasn't tough or mean. He was big on the group work that's at the heart of today's educational approach, though he tended to talk too much to be considered a flawless practitioner.

He and his students sometimes became noisily exuberant with a lesson. But he didn't let it go far, and at the hint of a serious disruption, he calmed things by swinging into a concerned tone of voice. He'd pretend to listen, though he much preferred to talk, trying to relate to the students by explaining the consequences of their actions for both good and bad. When he worked with the older kids on their college applications, he tried to make it as though they were all hanging out after school. But his style sometimes strayed too casual for Ms. P's cathedral of learning. He was, in many ways, so '70s.

Bookbinder and I were both products of a 1970s educational system that was far less data-driven than today's and more focused on building character and a love of learning. It may not have been that way everywhere, but it certainly was in the New York suburbs where Bookbinder and I grew up. For us, high school in particular was a wonderful place. There were homerooms and homework, as well as rigidity in math and science, but so much of the work didn't seem that way at all. The teachers challenged us, argued with us, and even became accomplices as we shot Super 8 movies and organized sign-waving demonstrations that were an outgrowth of our studies. By the time we were seniors in high school, we were so close to some of our teachers that we were almost on a first-name basis.

In addition to his old-school approach, Bookbinder had a bad case of having to speak. Whenever the lead teacher tried to explain something, if Bookbinder was in the room, he would attempt to hijack the topic by adding something. It quickly became obvious that the lead teacher hated him for that. Despite the talk of a collegial atmosphere, at Latinate there was a hierarchy, and it was to be observed by listening to those above you. Not speaking, just listening and implementing.

There also was a strong sense of not wasting the administration's time. Therefore, Bookbinder's tendency to prattle in the presence of the principal was practically a felony. I could feel Ms. P's impatience when Bookbinder said more than two consecutive sentences at a staff meeting. As did the lead teacher, Ms. P detested him.

"She gave me a U last year," Bookbinder told me when we first met. "She said, 'All I want from you is to have you out of my school.' She's jealous of my relationship with the kids, and she knows I could do her job far better than she does."

As a tenured teacher, Bookbinder couldn't be easily fired or transferred. Ms. P would have to get more on him than what she considered his grating personality. But with a U on his record, it was unlikely another school would have him. So Bookbinder and Ms. P were stuck together.

Another new member of the English Department was Ms. Nenza. Freshly minted with a master's of teaching, she was a tiny, thin twenty-four-year-old along the lines of actress Calista Flockhart. As an undergraduate, Ms. Nenza had attended the same state university I did—though decades later. One thing that hadn't changed in all of those years was the type of person New York's Binghamton University produced—a smart workaholic who is determined to prove that Binghamton and its graduates are the equals of any big-name school. That Binghamton was a big name among the Latinate faculty didn't seem to dawn on Ms. Nenza, and she jumped in immediately, working furiously to set up a classroom library and decorate her classroom.

Yes, she had a classroom. She got it by the luck of the draw. Or, more precisely, by the luck of her schedule of classes. Only a handful of teachers had rooms that they didn't have to share on more than a casual basis at Latinate. There were enough rooms for every teacher to be a sole resident, but that would have disrupted Ms. P's plan of segregating the students by grade level and keeping them confined to specific parts of each hallway.

The lead teacher, of course, had her own room—she made up

the teachers' schedules. Thus, so did the lead teacher's favorite, Ms. Snowden, a bright, cute young woman who had come to Latinate on the two-year Teach for America program.

I had the same classroom for three periods in the morning, but after that, I was a "traveling teacher." The way Ms. P had set up the school made most of us traveling teachers. Although Latinate consisted of just three short hallways that formed a T on the third floor of the old elementary school, she deemed that the halls—and students—should be segregated by grade level. Never mind that at the change of periods students of all ages came together in a crush of adolescent humanity at the joint of the T. Also, it seemed pointless to obsessively separate the students by age when so many were brothers and sisters and cousins of each other. But rather than have the students come to the teachers, most teachers had to come to the students, wheeling carts laden with books, papers, computers, and markers. It was a layer of hassle that, for me at least, made it tough to look and feel highly in charge and professional, especially when frantically trying to get to my next classroom while navigating hallways clogged with kids.

Having my own classroom would have been *luxurious*. Back in the corporate world, I'd had my own office for the past couple of decades. I'd be lying if I said the forty-third-floor views out to Central Park and the Hudson River weren't breathtaking, and the door that closed for privacy and escape wasn't a wonderful perk. But after arriving at Latinate, I would have happily traded all of the glass, carpet, and mahogany that had been lavished on me over the years in exchange for a stretch of linoleum tiles, beat-up desks, steel lockers, plastic whiteboards, and spring-loaded window shades that I could have called my own.

When I watched the lead teacher open the door for the two periods she taught each day, it was as though she were ushering the students into her personal salon. And in a way, it *was* a personal salon. There was no scurrying to get to class on time. No fretting about whether the Smart Board would work and whether the computer would be stolen, broken, or virus-infected. The desks, chairs, and whiteboard would be arranged exactly as she wanted them, exactly as she had left them.

That said, I could be wistful but certainly couldn't complain about not having a classroom when much more senior teachers, such as Ms. Lyons and Ms. Patel, were veritable itinerants of the Latinate hallways. Especially Ms. Patel, who was constantly on the move. In a school where the principal often cited issues with "my budget" and as a cost-containment measure limited teachers to two whiteboard markers at a time, an expensive, old-school teacher who had been thrust upon her wasn't welcome. Clearly, Ms. P was taking no chances—she wanted Ms. Patel off Latinate's budget, retiring when the clock struck twenty-five years, and if a U rating wasn't enough to do it, the dizzying commute among classrooms just might be.

To an outsider, moving among classrooms may not seem like much of a hardship. But then, to an outsider, teaching often looks easy. After all, don't you just stand in front of the room, ask the kids questions, and have them write the answers on the board? That, of course, is followed by July and August off.

Part of my training as a teacher involved fifty hours of observation at a high-needs school. Not student teaching, but watching pros in the classroom. Of course, watching is far different from doing. Like golf, tennis, and intimate acts, teaching looks quite easy when you see a skilled practitioner at work.

But when I entered the classroom myself to teach for the first time, I quickly realized that it's nowhere near as simple as that. Those of us who went to school when teachers lectured and students took notes are seen as educational dinosaurs. Talking, telling, and scrawling on the board are, quite literally, old school. If only teaching were as easy today as saying, "Take out your notebooks. Let's get started," and then launching into forty-six minutes on today's topic.

Instead, the twenty-first-century classroom is a laboratory of interaction and cooperative learning—*students learning from one another more than from the teacher*. The teacher is no more than the person who gathers the material for learning, sets the learning in motion, and then guides, nudges, and redirects the students who might veer off course for any number of reasons. While the class as a whole moves forward, the teacher must constantly consider each individual's emotional, educational, physical, and language needs, as well as each student's learning style, attention span, and previous work in this area, among many other factors, and adjust the individual instruction accordingly.

At a high-needs school, the challenges teachers face are even greater because the challenges so many of the children face are often greater. These range from poverty to hunger to undiagnosed and unmet medical and emotional needs to family and lack-of-family distractions to English being a very distant second language. As a result, calm, order, following authority, and self-control are foreign concepts to many of the students at high-needs schools because they often haven't been exposed to them previously or had these behaviors enforced or encouraged.

Granted, for all teenage kids—with their hormones running wild and high-fructose-fueled diets that can overwhelm their brains—calm, order, following authority, and self-control can be foreign concepts. But they are even more so at high-needs schools. So, while the teacher-as-facilitator and intensive individualized learning are noble and worthwhile goals, the first order of business is keeping some sort of order.

Among the most infamous of high-needs schools is the one I call Buchanan High School, where I did my training observation hours. Although set in the heart of suburban Long Island, the population of the town I call Buchanan is far from the affluent, white country-club set. The one-square-mile community is almost entirely black and Hispanic, and four in five students qualify for free or reduced-price lunches, a standard measure of poverty in student bodies.

After years of bad management, bad politics, and bad luck, Buchanan's schools were taken over by the state in 2002. The only one of more than 700 districts in New York to be placed under state control, Buchanan spent nearly a decade burning through hundreds of millions of dollars and a succession of state-appointed superintendents. The situation has started to turn around, but Buchanan High School is still a tough place.

While Buchanan's students lined up each morning at a metal detector in the foyer, I signed in with the security guards. After the first couple of times of making sure I didn't have any weapons in my briefcase, I was allowed to walk through uninspected. A large, well-worn relic of the 1970s, the school has linoleum floors and ceramic-tile walls in ugly earth tones. Posters notify the students of Picture Day and advertise various colleges that feature leafy campuses and smiling faces looking up from microscopes. At the end of the main hall is a man in a security uniform. In fact, there's a man in a security uniform on nearly every hall.

Although I visited other schools, other grades, and other teachers at Buchanan, I spent most of the academic year—and far more than my required fifty hours—in Mr. Russo's ninth-grade English class.

I met Mr. Russo as his students do—standing by the door to his classroom. These days, teachers don't sit at their desk with the grade book, waiting for the students to file in and be seated. During each period change, today's teacher stands by the door, welcoming the class, one by one. A short, well-muscled fellow in his mid-twenties, Mr. Russo wore a smile and a long-sleeved shirt and tie.

"Hello, Nahilia," he said.

"Hey, Charles."

He was friendly but not too familiar. There was firmness behind his manner that made it clear to the kids that they were supposed to get to work *right now*.

"The Do Now is on the board. Let's go."

The Do Now is the antipasto of the lesson. It's a little something to get the kids started and committed to staying for the main course. Mr. Russo's Do Nows typically asked the students to write down something from their own experience that related to the lesson to come. For instance, "Think about a time that you were tricked and how it felt." That might be the Do Now for a lesson on the short story "The Most Dangerous Game," in which the protagonist goes from being a guest to being the prey of a big-game hunter.

After letting them jot stuff down for a few minutes, Mr. Russo went around the room and called on various kids.

"A guy asked if he could use my phone, and then ran off with it."

"When we was at Splish Splash Water Park, my cousin said that this one ride was a kiddie ride. So I go on it with her, and 'AAAAAAA!' It was scary. I was crying, it was so scary. And my cousin was laughing and laughing."

"The guy at the Chinese place didn't give me all my change. He ripped me off for fifty cents!"

The kids started reading what they had written, but within seconds they were just telling the stories. And before Mr. Russo moved on to the next phase of the lesson, nearly a dozen kids had contributed.

This was Mr. Russo's first year full-time at Buchanan. After a year at a high school in the Bronx, he moved to a part-time position at Buchanan's night school, where returning dropouts, new mothers, and others who can't make the 8 a.m. to 3 p.m. school day take classes in the late afternoon or evening. The principal of the high school previously had been the principal of the night school. A long-time teacher and administrator in the district, the principal, now in her sixties, told me that Mr. Russo was "one of the very best." That's why he had been moved to full-time daytime duty.

Latinate's Ms. P, as well as the professors in my teacher-training program, would not have agreed. Mr. Russo was anything but the light hand guiding thirty cooperative learners in a creative exploration of state-recommended literature. There was a simple directness to his approach. Occasionally, he split the class up into small groups to work on a project for ten minutes or so, but for the most part he was the ringmaster of the classroom. Guiding the reading, leading the discussion, and being the disciplinarian.

"*Shhhh!*" he exhaled, raising his hand in a stop signal dozens of times each period. That sound and gesture, along with waiting for any perpetrators to stop perpetrating, usually was enough. But for some kids, that didn't work especially well.

Todd was a particularly hard case. Smart, often charming, and at least a year older than the other ninth graders, Todd already had a rap sheet with the cops for sexual assault. When a topic interested him, or he was permitted to be the star—reading aloud, telling a story, or performing in a play—he was cooperative. But otherwise, he was disruptive, calling out, throwing things, and whacking the kids around him with whatever was at hand. Though he was smiling, I always felt a dangerous tension not far beneath the surface.

"Todd, you have to go," Mr. Russo would say.

"No. Please!" said the pleading charmer.

"Go," the teacher said firmly, opening the classroom door.

As soon as Todd stepped into the hall, Mr. Washburne, the retired police officer who served as a uniformed security guard, intercepted him. Mr. Washburne took Todd to the room for those thrown out of class. Here, at any given time, a half-dozen or more students were sitting out the period in strictly enforced silence. The idea was to shame them. And it typically worked for most kids a couple of days at a time.

Tyrone was sent to the room occasionally when his attention deficit hyperactivity disorder got the best of him. At those times, he couldn't sit still, couldn't focus, and couldn't cope with the usual structures that kept him from acting out.

"It's a shame he's not classified," Mr. Russo sighed one day after class. "If he were classified, he could get some help."

By "classified" he meant being designated a special-education student. This classification can entitle a student, by law, to an individualized education program (IEP), a full range of individualized instruction, and even a special-ed teacher helping his regular teacher in each class. This classification can be a blessing to a child, giving him the help he needs to catch up with—and on occasion even zip ahead of—his peers.

"But his parents refuse to have him classified. They don't want him to have that stigma."

The result, of course, was that Tyrone didn't get the help he needed and he spent too much time either disrupting the class or being away from it.

Many of the other kids weren't disruptive at all. They were silent as they checked the texts on their cell phones by holding them under the desk or dropping them into recesses in their backpacks that sat on the floor or hiding the phones behind textbooks the way previous generations disguised comic books.

Karl, who didn't have a phone, talked to me. A thin, quiet kid in no-name jeans and logo-free sneakers, he had recently moved to Buchanan to live with his father. The other kids treated him as though he were invisible.

"How do you like Buchanan?" I asked.

"The breakfast was better at Elmont," he said. "They gave you a lot more and it was a lot better."

Like many of the kids, Karl lined up for the free breakfast in the cafeteria each morning. And like many of the kids, Karl was used to moving from one school district to another as he lived with a succession of family members. Some kids would cycle among various districts over their school career and sometimes even throughout the school year.

"I want to be an oral surgeon," he told me one day. "My aunt worked for an oral surgeon and they make lots of money."

While Karl quietly dreamed of his oral-surgery fortune, Mr. Russo pressed on and other students constantly fidgeted and looked for distractions. A sneeze could become a class project.

"Acchooo!"

"God bless you"

"God bless you."

"God bless you."

"God bless you."

"God bless you."

…and so forth, until just about everyone in the class had invoked the Almighty in an effort to push Mr. Russo off track.

"We're at the bottom of page 128," he calmly but firmly reminded them.

"I'm cold. Can't you close the window?" said a girl.

"Please read that paragraph at the bottom of page 128," he said to the chilly girl, distracting her back to the work at hand.

While she read, around the classroom cell phones were checked, lip balm was applied, tubes of skin moisturizer were passed as the kids constantly rubbed lotion on their hands and arms, and when they thought Mr. Russo wasn't looking, Skittles and Jolly Ranchers were tossed like surreptitious mackerel to seals at SeaWorld. Mr. Russo could have fought this behavior, but it seemed so ingrained in the kids that he would have had to constantly—and continually—chide and discipline members of the class. Any sort of schoolwork would have been replaced by a battle of wits. After all, even if a student is sitting quietly, it doesn't mean he or she is paying attention. Nor does an occasional airborne Skittle denote that no learning is taking place.

Like a good general, a good parent, or a good teacher, he knew that he couldn't and shouldn't fight every fight.

The more I observed Mr. Russo—and the more I observed other teachers at both Buchanan and other schools—the more I could see just how good he was. He wasn't a practitioner of state-of-the-art cooperative learning, but he was—given the circumstances—quite effective. While the kids fidgeted and looked for any excuse to get off topic, they seemed to like the class. Mr. Russo was able to power through the canon of ninth-grade English, from Guy de Maupassant to Frank McCourt, and ingrained in the students' brains concepts ranging from the "gothic story" (Edgar

Allan Poe's "The Cask of Amontillado") to literary terms such as "foil" and "onomatopoeia." He constantly reinforced what they had studied before—or reintroduced it to those who hadn't been paying attention the first couple of times—by bringing up "old" topics and quizzing the class.

"What's the conflict here: Man vs. man? Man vs. nature? Man vs. society? Or man vs. himself?"

The answers flew like so many Skittles as more than a dozen kids excitedly jumped in.

Yet it seemed to me that Mr. Russo wouldn't have earned a passing grade at Empire State College, where I was enrolled in the master's of teaching program.

"The lessons must be engaging!" my professor howled during our evening get-togethers. "You must engage the student!"

A short, round woman in her mid-40s, Dr. Kouffo was born in Benin, in West Africa, and attended college in both Ukraine and Georgia (the U.S. state) before teaching future teachers at Empire State. As far as I could tell, she never taught middle school or high school, but like many academics, she had strong opinions about how it should be done.

In this context, "engagement" meant more than students merely absorbing and even participating in what was going on in class. Engagement was sort of an educational rapture that brought all the kids in the class into deep emotional connection with the topic, the lesson, and their fellow students. It was the teacher's job to get them there.

Creativity, engagement, and empowering students to discover their "voice" were essential to any good pedagogic endeavor, per her advice. So, when the assignment was to create and present a lesson, I took Dr. Kouffo's mantra to heart and developed a lesson for ninth-grade English called "Citizen Journalism." This lesson required the class to break up into small groups. Each group would rate different brands of potato chips (which I supplied) based on saltiness, greasiness, crispness, and other factors. The groups would then write short reviews of the chips and post these on a blog, using a classroom computer.

When I tried this lesson out one evening on my Empire State classmates, my fellow graduate students loved it. Many had been at work all day, and a fistful of potato chips was the next best thing to dinner. Dr. Kouffo was beside herself with delight. She loved the chips; she loved the ratings; she loved my use of "technology"; she loved the engagement. When the greasy fingers and salty palates had settled, I had scored a solid A.

Some weeks later, Mr. Russo was heading out of town for a three-day conference. He asked if I would fill in at ninth-grade English.

"You bet," I said. "And I have a lesson plan I would like to try out."

I didn't do the potato-chip Citizen Journalism lesson on Day 1, figuring it was best to segue slowly from Mr. Russo's presence. We continued reading *Romeo and Juliet* aloud in class. There also was something of a pall cast over the class, since the day before he left, Mr. Russo had berated the ninth graders long and loud because someone had come into the classroom when he wasn't there and thrown the various dollar-store plastic swords that were our Shakespearean props out the window.

"Fortunately, I saw them outside on the grass and brought them in," he angrily told the students.

By Day 2, I figured that feuding families and star-crossed

lovers were creating enough trouble for the kids, so I let them continue reading aloud and fencing with the plastic swords.

Immediately after class, there was a huge clamor in the hallway where two of the kids from my class were going at it in heads-slamming-against-the-wall fury. There was blood. There were screams. There were Mr. Washburne and other blue-uniformed security guards rushing down the hall and pushing their way through the knot of whooping, cheering, and yelling onlookers. Soon, the two students were being dragged past my classroom, seething in anger.

"It's gang related," Mr. Washburne told me as he passed, his right arm firmly gripping one kid's bicep and wrist.

I silently thanked these modern-day Montagues and Capulets for waiting until class was over.

On Day 3, I left the potato chips at home. The wisdom of my decision was reinforced by the splatters of blood I found on the classroom floor. As with the plastic swords that had gone out the window the previous week, there were no witnesses. I just rearranged the desks so none of us had to step in the blood and pressed on with *Romeo and Juliet*.

I could see that we were a long way from breaking into small groups and rating potato chips. Disturbing the usual pattern of the class would have given the kids the sense that this was a free period, and with the introduction of food, their excitement definitely would have escalated it into a free-for-all period. Not the sort of thing I was willing—or able—to handle. And so, I stuck to the tried and true, recognizing that their regular teacher was very smart, very good, and very practical. There were many sound reasons for why he wasn't getting much more creative in his lesson plans than bringing in plastic swords. I left Mr. Russo a nice note thanking him for letting me fill in.

Like Buchanan's principal, I could see that Mr. Russo was a very effective teacher. As with teachers everywhere—in schools ranging from high needs to high income—he was unable to quiet, calm, and academically focus every student every second of the period. That's reality. Yet, Mr. Russo's approach would have put him deep in U territory at Latinate. All Ms. P would need to see would be an airborne Skittle, a stealth check of a cell phone, or a yawn from a kid bored with Romeo's *"See, how she leans her cheek upon her hand! O that I were a glove upon that hand, that I might touch that cheek!"*

Like Ms. P, America is demanding too much from its teachers without giving them the proper support to educate students effectively. Commitment, caring, pushing for results, and putting in a full work's day no longer seem to be enough. Today, teachers must be able to pull every student into every topic with the power of a video game and get them to not only absorb but also to process, analyze, and synthesize the information at the highest level. And do it every day, every time, regardless of the students' learning abilities or the resources available to them. The general expectation is that poverty, learning disabilities, medical-emotional issues, and behavior problems shouldn't stand in the way of student achievement. But unfortunately, as the next chapter demonstrates, they do.

MY STUDENTS AND ME

Fewer than a third of eighth graders read and write at a proficient level (that is, at a level deemed to be appropriate for their year in school). And for low-income students and students of color, the statistics are even more alarming: just 13 percent of African-American, 17 percent of Hispanic, and 15 percent of low-income eighth graders were found to be proficient in reading.

—U.S. Department of Education, National
Assessment of Educational Progress, 2007

WHAT THE FUCK, MISTER?" the tenth grader snarled. "What the fuck you doing scoping me down there?"

"Put the phone away," I stated firmly, now in my second full day as a teacher at Latinate. "Put the phone away."

Natasha had stuffed her cell phone between the khaki-colored legs of her Latinate Institute uniform pants. She accused me of seeing the phone only because I was checking out her crotch. But I wasn't intimidated by her diversion.

"Put the phone away, Natasha. Now."

"You a fuckin' pervert, mister."

A big laugh from the class.

Tall and appearing much older than any tenth grader I had ever seen, Natasha possessed a well-practiced, mixed look of anger and disgust. I never saw her anywhere—in class, in the hall, on the sidewalk after school—looking anything but angry and disgusted. She was among a quartet of girls who were taking tenth-grade English for the second or third time. And from the way things were going already during the first days of school, there was a good chance they'd have another go-round.

Although Natasha and her posse created a great deal of noise and bounced around the room like mean-spirited medicine balls, I was determined not to let them overshadow the other students or disrupt their learning.

There was Nora, the quiet, studious girl who had moved from Georgia several years before, and who still believed that her job was to listen to the teacher, do the class assignments, and have her homework ready the next day. She looked like a young Michelle Obama, and her old-fashioned approach, bright smile, and modest hair and makeup always brought to mind the good teenage daughter in a TV sitcom.

And there was Lester, whose parents had emigrated from West Africa and who displayed discipline and respect for learning that established an instant rapport between us. He was bright and articulate, and could pull meaning out of a poem as if he were reaching into a grab bag. But as a thoroughly Americanized kid, he also was willing to be distracted from his work. Though rather than start checking his cell phone or banging the desk to accompany a spontaneous rap, Lester liked to talk to me and the students in a manner that reminded me so much of Johnny Carson that I was expecting Ed McMahon to pop through the classroom door at any moment.

"I see you have a can of Diet Pepsi on your cart," Lester

said with the ease of a talk-show host, as he nodded toward the contraption I used to travel from classroom to classroom. "Don't worry about me taking it. Black people only drink grape soda."

This garnered not quite a laugh, but an appreciative chuckle from the other good students. Yet later, as I wheeled my cart out the classroom, I noticed that the can of soda had vanished.

Of course, most of the class didn't hear Lester's remark since they were stealthily checking their phones, rapping, or frowning at another kid across the room and saying, "Suck my dick, nigga." That, in turn, would incite the other kid to jump up, dart over to his opponent, and shout, "Suck my dick, nigga!" in his face. Still, nothing even approached the Natasha Gang.

As I had been told to do, I used the online reporting system to give the girls detention and report their activities to the dean. Within a few days, I had typed a thick electronic file on Natasha & Co. that was dense with reports of "foul language" and "disrupting the educational process." The dean told me that although detention hadn't yet gotten under way for the school year, she had spoken to the girls. However, I couldn't discern any difference in their noise, disruptions, and dancing around the classroom.

Like me, the dean was new to the school, and one lunch period, I stopped by her office, a former closet next to the girls' restroom. A bright, down-to-earth woman in her early thirties who lived with her husband and kids in the South Bronx, she told me that she had moved from being a teacher to start her climb up the educational hierarchy, with the plan of someday being a principal. Although the school year was still young, she already was overloaded with discipline problems. The Natasha Gang was just one of many.

"What can I do?" I asked.

She sighed and had just started an "I don't know" shrug that suggested she had done all she was going to do for me when her phone rang, and she gestured me out.

I called whatever parents of the four I could find, but as with many of the students at Latinate, their parents seemed to be in the witness protection program. They were impossible to locate, at least from what teachers said. Some parents used only prepaid cell phones. And when that phone was used up, the number went bad. I encountered that many times.

Sometimes the parents gave the school a phone number that had nothing to do with them or their lives. It was just something to complete the paperwork. When I reached everything from an optometrist's office to annoyed night-shift workers who were trying to sleep, I realized that the parents were, as the kids would say, "playin' wit choo." I received thick printouts of phone numbers, addresses, names of family members, and other "student data" that contained as much fiction as any story we read in class.

Sometimes there were no parents. There might be aunts, grandmothers, or an ever-changing succession of people, most of whom definitely didn't want to hear from a teacher. Other times there were parents or other family members who cared a great deal. But they just didn't know what to do to get their kids to behave, do the work, or do anything else constructive.

That was exactly what I heard from Mr. Rashid, a short, wiry African immigrant who visited me at school in work clothes covered in soot. His daughter Zanatala was part of the four-girl classroom wrecking crew headed by Natasha. When the school's guidance counselor and I spoke to him, all he could say was, "I know. But I just don't know what to do." I didn't know what to do, either.

Despite a year of graduate-level teacher-prep classes, I wasn't prepared for this. I was struggling with developing lessons for these tenth graders, gathering the data required by the principal, and calling whichever adults in these kids' lives I could find. Determining what to do about kids whose serious behavior problems stymied their parents was beyond my training and experience. Other teachers were sympathetic but not much help. Early in the school year, we all were dealing with so much tumult and change and paperwork that nobody had much time or the attention span for anything other than their own problems.

Although the guidance counselor told me that she, too, had spoken with Natasha, Zanatala, & Co. after other teachers reported discipline issues with them, from all indications, these girls were *my* problem. Not just teaching them and boosting their academic achievement, but also managing whatever issues they had so that they could achieve.

I felt a wave of impotence wash over me as Mr. Rashid turned and left.

According to the principal, behavior and discipline issues in the classroom were the teacher's responsibility. In other words, asking for backup was bad form. However, each class at Latinate was incredibly diverse in terms of both the kids' individual academic skills and their behavior. The results were wild cards and wild kids in every class. Some were much older than the others because they were taking the class for the second or third time. Some were much farther behind because they were special-education students.

Some—such as Alec, a tall, frequently out-of-control, sixteen-year-old ninth grader who had recently arrived from the Dominican Republic—both were classified special ed and possessed no English language skills whatsoever. This mix was deliberate, part of the aforementioned trend in teaching called "cooperative learning." This approach puts students of various levels together in one classroom, and the academically strong kids help the academically weak ones.

"They learn more from each other than they will ever learn from you," is the mantra of cooperative learning. The idea is to put the kids in carefully chosen groups or pairings, give them very specific assignments with highly detailed instructions, and then guide them with a firm but nearly invisible hand. The students help each other, evaluate each other's ideas and contributions, and use each other's skills and strengths to the group's advantage. At least that's the theory.

In addition to students helping students, the teacher is supposed to give various students various assignments of different levels, an approach called "differentiated instruction." In schools throughout New York City and throughout the country, this approach is to be used in *every* lesson in every imaginable topic and subject. From botany to basketball and from cosines to Shakespeare, you're not teaching if you're not using skill-building cooperative learning and differentiated instruction. And don't forget various learning styles. Some kids learn best by listening. Others by reading. Others taking a hands-on approach. Some learn by coloring; just don't call it "coloring." That doesn't have the ring of academic rigor.

To follow the school's mantra, I implemented this learning approach right from the start. One of the first assignments I gave my classes was to describe how to tie a tie. A plaid necktie was part of the Latinate uniform for both boys and girls, and not wearing the tie was said to be a serious infraction, so I figured this would be a fairly basic exercise to start, and it would let the students who had mastered the skill teach those who hadn't. But as my ninth grader Rikkie showed, few of the kids actually knew how to tie one. Most of them didn't come from families where anyone wore a tie, and for many, this school tie was the first tie in the family.

Using the skill-building cooperative learning and differentiated instruction techniques I learned in my master's of teaching program, I demonstrated tying a tie and then had the kids work with each other to master it. In each class, the result was the same: total confusion. Demonstrating it once never was enough. Nor twice. I became a tie-tying demonstration machine, walking around the room, providing individual lessons in how "the fat side goes over the thin side, and then up through the back and down through the hole."

I then asked the students to write the process in a step-by-step fashion. Those who had trouble writing could draw. Those who couldn't write it or draw it could simply show me how they tie a tie. And those who could do none of the above were to keep trying. There were many kids in each camp. After about half an hour, most of them could do it. There were laughs and hoots as they did it or didn't and kept at it.

"The fat side goes down through the hole," kids called to each other in a snickering tone that inevitably put a sexual spin on knotting a tie.

"Yeah, the hole."

The cooperative learning approach predates my career in education by many years, but the only time I saw it work well at Latinate was with fourteen-year-old Ahmad, and his best friend Mark, the ninth-grade all-American kid who was known as "a brain."

Born in Djibouti, a poor, tiny country on the Horn of Africa, Ahmad and his parents made their way to France when he was eight years old. After several years, they moved to the Bronx. Ahmad's facility with language amazed me. Not only did he speak Arabic (the language of his parents), but also French, and after just a few years in the United States, he spoke English like a native. Flawless. Hesitation- and accent-free. Short, thin, and with a face younger than his age, Ahmad was undeniably cute. And that made him a favorite victim for the tougher kids around him. He was the kind of kid whose pencils, notebooks, and even homework weren't his own if anyone—male or female—of larger stature or more aggressive manner wanted them.

Whether consciously or as the result of the fortunate attraction of opposites who really have much in common, on his first day of ninth grade—and his first day at Latinate—Ahmad teamed up with Mark, who also was new to the school. Although they were so different in many ways—for one, Mark was a couple of feet taller than Ahmad—they quickly became inseparable.

They came to school together, always arriving in my homeroom soon after the security people unwrapped the chains on the downstairs doors at 7:55 and the other kids were released from the cafeteria after receiving their city-sponsored breakfast. Only Pashima, the pink-clad future Mrs. Justin Bieber, beat them to my homeroom. Ahmad immediately offered to do any of the sorting, collecting, or chair-rearranging chores that come with homeroom; Mark typically reined him in.

"Ahmad, have you done all of your homework?" he'd ask, making the "give-it-to-me" motion. History, math, French—Mark reviewed them, checking his friend's work. English? Absolutely. Ahmad wrote the eighty-word essays each day. Okay, they often weren't the full eighty words. But forty words on "If I could change my name to anything, what name would it be?" at least showed some interest and effort. Vocabulary and spelling? When Ahmad studied—that is, when Mark prodded him—he did well, often getting eight or nine out of ten. But without the concerted effort, his vocabulary tests would be the nadir of lexicographic acuity.

"Hey, how come I didn't get any bonus points on the test?" Ahmad demanded of me when he saw that his score didn't match Mark's 110.

"Well," I said, charmed by his indignation. "You obviously didn't study. And getting the extra-credit question doesn't mean much when you get nine out of the first ten wrong."

Inevitably, Mark would give him a scowl of disapproval and a slap on the arm that said, "See, you should study more."

Aside from Mark and Ahmad, however, I didn't see a lot of successful cooperative learning at Latinate. For all the process and jargon of this style, I often wondered how much real learning went on. I wasn't alone. At least one parent decided that her son had gained nothing from Latinate's approach and took legal action against the school.

"Be careful," the assistant principal told me one September afternoon, shortly after the school year began. I had brought up the topic of Nestor, an out-of-control eighth grader. Suddenly, the assistant principal's tone became confidential. "His mother is suing the school. So be careful," he said softly.

Her complaint was that Nestor wasn't getting the education he deserved. By the time I met him, I couldn't discern much education at all. A tall, handsome, athletic-looking kid, Nestor resembled a high school football hero. But in reality, he was just an eighth-grade wild man. It became obvious to me that he acted up because he couldn't do anything we were covering in class; in short, he seemed to have a severe learning disability or attention disorder. Whether the assignment was vocabulary words or reading a simple short story, Nestor couldn't or wouldn't do the work.

I tried to push him toward simpler tasks, such as word searches and other basic literary puzzles that used his style of learning and would help him feel a sense of achievement alongside the other students. But instead of doing the work, Nestor liked to approach me at the front of the classroom and throw punches toward my face. Pulling back just before he connected with my mouth or letting his fists fly by so close that I could smell his lunch on his hands, Nestor wanted to see if I would flinch.

"Be careful!" The assistant principal's admonition about Nestor's litigious mother kept me ignoring the punches from a kid who was not only taller and faster than me, but also had better legal representation.

Later in the year, another lawsuit against the school hit the papers. A boy who had left the school months before was suing for a civil rights violation. The fifteen-year-old eighth grader claimed he didn't receive grades while he was attending Latinate, but months after he had transferred out, he not only got a report card but had an online progress report, too. In fact, the *New York Daily News* reported that transcripts showed him "enrolled in four...classes he never took, taught by teachers he never had."

Ms. P quickly got to the root of the problem. "The teachers must be more careful in recording grades," she admonished us at a staff meeting shortly after the news broke.

Clearly, incidents like this reflected poorly on the school and the accuracy of the grades or any other data coming out of Latinate, but the assistant principal would only allow that such matters "took up a lot of the administration's time." And he repeatedly made it clear to the teachers that in everything we did—especially when talking to parents—we should never let any situation get to the point where it required the administration's time.

After a couple weeks of taunting me, Nestor turned to putting his hand down the front of his pants, sticking his fist out the fly, and menacing girls in the class with it.

"My dick is gonna get you!" Nestor shouted as he bounded up and down the aisles of the eighth-grade classroom, poking screeching girls with his phallic fist.

"Finally!" I said to myself as I filed the report on his sexual harassment.

Soon after, Nestor was jumped and beaten up by a group of older boys, and his mother transferred him to another school.

I felt bad about Nestor's beating and the likelihood that his new school would be no better at providing the education he really needed. Instead of receiving intensive special-education and mental-health services, chances are Nestor would just be thrown into another eighth-grade class where he would learn nothing, disrupt the learning of the other kids, and make the teacher's life miserable. In addition, he would pull down the test scores and other data that determined the efficacy of his teacher and school. A sad situation. But I couldn't help feeling rather relieved to have him out of my class.

Even in the ninth-grade writing workshop, where the "disruptions" were mostly of the positive kind as kids called out answers without raising their hands and argued about the lesson topic, the range of students—and their abilities—was staggering. I had set up the class as a true workshop, where everyone was a writer—there were no exceptions. But for some of these students, even assuming that identity for forty-six minutes a day was a challenge.

"Infiniti, what's your title?" I bellowed, pointing my finger at the young girl.

"Writer."

"Almon, what is your title?" I said, spinning around, pointing toward the boy sitting on the other side of the room.

"Ah, writer?" he said tentatively.

"Sarah. Your title."

"Writer," she said brightly, her smile broad.

"Shaneblane, what's your title?" I asked.

"Shaniqua's baby daddy," he said, beaming with the knowledge that he probably would never say anything this clever again.

"You stay away from me, Shaneblane," Shaniqua squealed from several rows away.

"Well, Shaneblane, at least you have a writer's imagination," I said when the whoops and yells and high fives had died down, only to start again at my cheeky remark.

From homeroom through the first three periods, I had ninth graders in the writing workshop. Since the state recognizes that reading and writing are core skills in everything from science to social studies—and a key part of the state exams—the ninth graders received two periods of English each day—one focused on reading, the other on writing. I handled writing; Ms. Nenza, the newly minted master of teaching, taught reading.

New York State standards dictated that students be adept at "using evidence to support ideas" and "demonstrating awareness of audience." But I also knew that I had to deal with such basics as "capitalizing sentence starters and proper nouns" and "ending sentences with appropriate punctuation" in order for them to achieve that. I figured these were among the basic skills the assistant principal had mentioned when he hired me.

During my teacher-observation at Buchanan High School, I encountered many kids in mainstream high school classes who were barely literate and not engaged enough in their education for that to change anytime soon. It was a dose of reality that underscored how teaching basic skills really was a major part of the job.

Ms. Farner, an excellent English teacher whom I observed at

Buchanan and whose classroom was next door to Mr. Russo's, asked her ninth graders to sit in a circle and read aloud the children's book *Faithful Elephants* by Yukio Tsuchiya. Set in World War II, it's the story of how the zookeepers at Tokyo's Ueno Zoo poisoned the large, dangerous animals that might escape and endanger the public if bombs fell on the zoo. The poison, however, didn't work on three Indian elephants. So these creatures were starved to death. Sad stuff. A heartbreaking book.

Ms. Farner asked the students to react to it and tell whether they thought it was appropriate reading for young children. There were several thoughtful responses such as this one:

> Innocent animals suffer because of human warfare. I believe they could have done something better than kill the animals. What do they know about war? They know nothing. They know they have people who care about them. Why should the elephants suffer? They deserved to live. Even during the war, they could have sought out a solution. This book is very sad, but it is appropriate for little children because it teaches them what war is and who it can affect.

But most responses were along the lines of these:

> "That was wrong all you had to do was shout them or send them to a safe zoo to go to."
> "Also people needs to move somewhere thats more safer."
> "I think they had to kill the animals they wanted to kill them All they had to do was yous the animals in the war."

"Hey I guess it was time 4 them to die But too bad
so sad."

When I walked into Latinate after observing that at Buchanan,
I knew we were going to have to spend a good deal of time building foundations in basic English language skills, and I also knew
that I would have to find a way to make the majority of these kids
care about this class. If a wonderful, experienced teacher and a
tear-jerking story of starving elephants couldn't elicit more from
students than a couple haphazardly spelled and carelessly punctu-
ated sentences, anything approaching the "literary analysis" that
was required by the state standards was going to be an impossibly
tough slog for a beginner like me.

Obviously, these kids had other things on their minds. Some faced
issues far larger than carefully crafting assignments. According to
Newsday, the Long Island newspaper, one-square-mile Buchanan
reported eighty-four police incidents—including three homicides
and eight robberies, in a twelve-month period—while the New
York State Division of Criminal Justice Services listed nearly
two dozen registered sex offenders among its 16,000 residents.
Poverty? I imagined that some of these students were not far from
being starving elephants themselves.

Latinate's neighborhood, the 42nd Precinct in the South Bronx,
had even more gruesome statistics, with the New York City Police
Department reporting eight murders, twenty rapes, 254 robberies,
994 assaults, and twenty-nine misdemeanor sex crimes in 2011.
And those numbers represented improvements over prior years.

Considering the world around my students at Latinate, I

thought it was important for them to have a very special and very strong identity in my class. As writers, they might get more involved and invested in the course, as well as understand the importance of mastering basic grammar, spelling, and punctuation skills.

"Okay," I said on the first day of class at Latinate, "take the piece of paper that I have handed out and write your name on it, followed by the word 'writer.'"

I wanted each student to have a tent card—a piece of stiff paper that is folded in half to form a tent—on the desk with his or her name on it, followed by the title, Writer.

"You just want us to do this so you don't have to memorize our names," said a smart-ass whose name I didn't know.

"That's half right," I admitted, laughing.

Yes, it partially helped me learn their names, which was going to take a while: Almon, A'Don, Macon, Niezia, Sharleny, Sarize, Devon, Saquaan, Shaniqua, Janiel, Marneyis, and Stephan (pronounced "Sta-FON"), to name a few. I come from a long line of Johns, and such boring names are familiar and easy for me. But among my 125 students in five classes, there was only one John, one James, one Jason. Such old-school names don't make much sense to these kids. At Buchanan High School, we read Richard Connell's short story "The Most Dangerous Game." The protagonist is a man named Whitney. The kids thought that was ridiculously funny.

"*Whitney?*" one boy shouted, laughing hard. "What kind of name is that for a man?"

Whitney—as in Whitney Houston—was a feminine name, everyone agreed.

"That's not a real man's name," a girl opined.

"No, it's a real boy's name," another girl said, her hilarity almost driving her to tears. "My aunt's dog is named Whitney."

Get a kid's name wrong—or even pronounce it slightly off—and the whole class could rise up in indignation. It wasn't a mistake; it was an affront. An insult. Disrespect. I understood that many of these kids had little more than their name, and so they took it very, very seriously. So with the writer exercise, I wanted not only to get their names right, but also to help them create identities they could carry with them anywhere.

It also was immediately clear that just as with tying a tie, getting through virtually every task would be a big deal. One of the few practical things we learned in the five days of new-teacher orientation at Latinate was that some high school students don't know left from right. Or can't tell time. But rather than say they don't know how to do it, they get hostile, lashing out at the teacher and refusing to do the task.

What appears as anger is often really frustration, and a reluctance to admit not knowing something that to other kids seems so simple—like telling time by reading the hands on a clock or knowing left from right or folding a piece of paper lengthwise. It wasn't a mental handicap so much as a gap in their knowledge. For many of these kids, no one had ever taught them and reinforced these concepts.

I saw this frustration when we tried to fold the paper into tent cards. The concept of creasing a piece of paper lengthwise—"the long way"—was more than some could grasp. And then writing their name and leaving space for the word "writer" was a similar brainteaser. In each class, I was patient, using words, visuals, and hands-on demonstrations to guide the kids through the folding and name-writing process. It's what educators call "adjusting to various learning styles."

For several students, I did it for them. That's called "modeling," or as a layman might say, "doing it for them." Okay, I admit that strictly speaking, modeling requires the student to then mimic exactly what you showed them, but just minutes into the school year, I could see that there had to be a limit to patience, and I felt that it wasn't a good investment of time to hold up the whole class for a handful of kids who hadn't mastered folding paper the long way.

The bottom line: the skills of my students ranged from those barely able to follow directions to bright, eager, well-prepared, college-bound high school freshmen, with most somewhere in between. It was evident early on that Ron—a big, happy kid who looked a bit like Magic Johnson—was far ahead of the rest of the class.

"Why are we doing this?" he asked when I put the narrative arc up on the Smart Board. "We did this in sixth grade."

"Well, it's just a refresher," I said, watching the kids copy the terms "exposition," "rising action," "climax," "falling action," and "denouement" into their notebooks like the words were part of a mathematical formula written in Martian. In fact, only Ron giggled pruriently when I said "climax." To almost everyone else, this was virgin territory. ("Virgin. Tee-hee.")

When I announced that we were going to cover vocabulary words ("Words are the tools a writer uses"), Ron sighed audibly at the lameness of such words as "excerpt" and "servile."

"Wow, Ron really got a great education at the school he went to before," I said to his mother, delighted when I could make a complimentary call to a parent.

"Well, I hope he is getting a good education where he is now," she countered.

I hesitated, wanting to tell her, "Get this kid the hell out of here!" but that would be an instant U when it got back to the principal. Instead, I just told her we were trying to give him the best education we could and that it sure was impressive how much he contributed in class and how far ahead of the other kids he was. *Hint. Hint.*

"Oh, my Ronnie. He loves to contribute in class," Mom said proudly.

Of course, I had to rein in Ron's contributions; otherwise no one else would get a chance. And when faced with the two of us, the Ron and Mr. Owens Show, I knew that the other students would cash in their emotional investment in the course and resort to passing the period by checking their phones and taunting kids across the room.

Ron landed at Latinate through a distinctively New York process. Midway through the eighth grade, New York City public school students begin applying to various high schools in the city. The high schools review the seventh-grade standardized test scores in math and reading, academic grades in all subject areas, and records of attendance and punctuality. Spots in the most famous and academically demanding schools (Bronx Science, Stuyvesant, Brooklyn Latin) are often filled by future Ivy Leaguers and tomorrow's Nobel Prize winners who excel on the city's Specialized High Schools Admission Test.* Other public schools jostle at recruiting fairs and in promotional material and meetings to draw the best students they can.

---

*The odds, however, are decidedly against Ron, Mark "the brain," or even eighth-grade super-student Santos attending one of these elite public high schools. As the NAACP pointed out in a September 2012 complaint to the U.S. Department of Education, only one percent of the students at Stuyvesant High School are black. Of the students taking the admission test for the city's eight elite schools, blacks and Latinos are denied admission "at rates far higher than other racial groups," said the complaint. Nearly 31 percent of white students and 35 percent of Asian students who take the test are accepted, compared with just 5 percent of black students and 6.7 percent of Latinos. City officials, however, insist that the process is color-blind.

Latinate, however, couldn't be choosy. Given its third-floor-walkup location, B overall grade, and numerous negative online reviews, the school took virtually all comers. Ron was so far beyond the other students in his class that I figured somehow in selecting where he would attend ninth grade—and probably all of high school—Ron's mom must have been blinded by the single-minded "college preparatory" pitch at Latinate Institute and missed the part about "kids who otherwise wouldn't go to college." Which, of course, was code for "lots of these kids otherwise wouldn't graduate from high school."

While many of the kids at Latinate lived in the nearby projects ("Don't call them the Projects," said one student who lived there. "Say 'the Tall Buildings'"), Ron was from a bit farther north in the Bronx, which has some wealthier, more suburban neighborhoods. His mother dropped him off at school every morning as she drove to her job in Manhattan. He always had an expensive deli-purchased breakfast that he picked up on the way.

"I'm so impressed with Ron," I said to his mother in one of my "Hint, hint, get him outta this school" conversations. "If he keeps his academics up to the level they have been, I wouldn't be surprised if someday we're all working for Ron."

His classmates included Shaneblane, who would have trouble distinguishing the narrative arc from Noah's ark. As a simultaneous ninth, tenth, and eleventh grader, Shaneblane took a dog's breakfast of courses that I suspect he had taken several times before as part of Ms. P's credit-recovery program.

Shaneblane tended to wander around the school at will when he was supposed to be in class, unmolested by the assistant principal, dean, assistant dean, school aide, or security people. Word was out that he was a favorite of the principal, and she was wont to hug him when passing in the hall. But when he was in my class,

I was supposed to keep him from disrupting the educational process by discussing how he would like to impregnate various girls
in the room, drawing penises on anything that wasn't moving, and
jumping around like a cash-rich street king, flashing a stack of
one-dollar bills. His short attention span, need to be noticed, and
lack of ability to do any of the classwork—along with his status
as a "principal's pet" —made me Shaneblane's third-period atten-
dant, while I simultaneously tried to be a teacher to his classmates.

After we got our cards folded and our names—or something
approaching our names—written on them, I gave each student
a sheet of paper that showed what appeared to be a big, smiling lightbulb. Above it was written "My Big Brain: What's on My
Mind." It was a getting-to-know-each-other exercise shared with
me by Barbara Jennes, a brilliant and experienced teacher I never
worked with but who is a longtime friend. Also a career-changer
who switched from writing to teaching, Barbara was a person to
whom I frequently turned for mentoring, support, and inspiration
during my brief teaching career.

Using Barbara's My Big Brain template, I printed a batch at
home on my inkjet printer. I thought it would be a good introduction to perspective and the unit on personal narrative. But more
immediately, I wanted to engage the kids with a topic they cared
about—*themselves.*

"Decorate this Big Brain with words, drawings, photos, stuff
torn out of magazines," I said enthusiastically. "The idea so to
show what *you* think about and what *you* care about. Start now,
but I want you to do this tonight as homework and hand it in
finished tomorrow."

Some of the class got busy right away, giving their brand-new
school supplies a workout. Markers, colored pens, colored pencils, and Wite-Out flew as the industrious and creative expressed

themselves. Others spent the rest of the period asking me lots of questions about the assignment and worrying that they could not possibly express what was in their brains and on their minds.

Given the opportunity to draw a penis, Shaneblane didn't. Instead, he got up and left the room.

"I gotta pee," he said on his way out. Before the door clicked shut behind him, I turned to the other students and encouraged their efforts.

If you listen to the administrators and other educational sages, the problem with students like Nestor, Natasha, and Shaneblane is that their teachers don't know how to engage them, or at least control them. And while nobody else knew what to do with Natasha and her foul-mouthed, singing, dancing, music-blasting posse, my immediate supervisor, the lead teacher, had the answer.

"Whenever there is trouble, you need to rearrange the seats," she said. "You have to assign them *new* seats."

So the next time the tenth-grade English class met, I lined everyone up against the lockers. Everyone that is, except Natasha and her posse, who refused to get out of their seats. Then, one by one I pointed the twenty-four other students to their new seats. Within seconds, the class broke into a Moroccan souk of negotiation, refusal, counteroffers, and vociferous outrage.

Only a few kids took their assigned seats. The rest were having great fun giving me a hard time. My new seating assignments coincided with a visit from the principal, Ms. P, who stood by with her arms folded, her mouth set in a sour grimace, and her long, thin eyebrows bouncing up and down as though they were skinny caterpillars on a trampoline.

"What was that you were trying to do?" she asked the next day in her office, not waiting for my answer. "Assign the children seats?"

My effort at class management was dismissed for what it was—a total failure.

I explained the problem with Natasha, Zanatala, and the others. I told her about detention, dean's referrals, and my conversation with Mr. Rashid. She just waved her hand.

"You need to have lunch with the girls," she said. "You need to show them that you care about them. Then they will behave in your class."

"Okay," I said agreeably, seeing that Ms. P was blissfully ignoring how angry and out of control these girls were. As I saw it, we were a long way off from lunching together. The dean had talked to the girls. So had the guidance counselor. Neither had made any positive impact. Some visits to a psychologist would have been far more useful to these kids than dining with Mr. Owens.

Nonetheless, I considered how to do this. Lunch in the cafeteria was a bad idea. That would give the girls an audience. So if they decided not to cooperate, they could make me look quite foolish. If they cooperated, they could make it look as though they and their antics held so much power that teachers were forced to make peace with them. We also couldn't go out to lunch. Taking students—especially these girls—out of the building was an invitation to anything from them beating the hell out of me to saying I tried to sexually assault them to simply disappearing. I didn't want any of that on my watch.

That meant a classroom lunch. Having the cafeteria send up something was out of the question. All they ever sent up to the third floor were peanut butter and jelly sandwiches. There was a school policy about letting anything more appealing out of the cafeteria. So I would have to have lunch brought in. Pizza, probably. I sensed Ms. P would rather not be involved in such minutiae as who would pay for it, so I reckoned I would have to spring for it.

Then I tried to wrap my brain around the logistics:

> I can't have the pizza delivered during the lunch period, because if it's even a little late in getting here, I'll have the four angry, hungry girls, and we might be pressed for time to discuss anything.... So I'll order it for fourth period, when I have lunch.... But don't the girls have lunch fifth period? Oh, wait, I have a class fifth period.... Should I get another teacher to cover for me? But then that class is losing its teacher because these four girls from another class can't behave...

As a journalist, I had eagerly dined with snooty British nobles, ruthless CEOs, and famously temperamental entertainers, yet as a teacher, I kept putting off pizza with these girls. I told myself I was still performing the mental gymnastics of organizing the meal, though I really was afraid. Afraid that this quartet—which couldn't be tamed by any experienced administrator in the school and had more than a decade of dealing with the System—would see me for what I was: a new teacher who was just trying to shut them up and sit them down. They could, I figured, devour me.

Would a couple of slices and a cup of soda convince them that I, as Ms. P mandated, "cared about them"? I doubted they were that naïve. Yet kids who are so outrageous typically are emotionally needy, and perhaps the girls would welcome someone who would listen to them, console them, and commiserate with them while plying them with pizza. But for a guy still in the first days of a new career, it was a mighty big risk.

As I continued to battle these thoughts—and battle the girls in my tenth-grade class—Ms. P lost patience and transferred the eighth graders to me. Mr. Bookbinder got the tenth graders.

"He had those students last year," Ms. P told me when she called me into her office. "He has a good relationship with those children."

Mr. Bookbinder—in a rare moment with little to say— nodded that it was true. Maybe he did have a good relationship with those students. Or maybe he was making this trade to get on Ms. P's good side. Or maybe he was doing this to prove he was worth far more than the Unsatisfactory rating he had received last year. I didn't know the answers, and I already had channeled enough mental horsepower into the problem of Natasha & Co. to have nothing left for the politics of the English Department. All I knew was that it was good-bye to these hellions and hello, new students.

That a teacher can spend so much time, energy, and emotion on the outrageous kids at the expense of the students who are making some academic effort is a common complaint of the profession. For new teachers who don't have the skills and experience to deal with the troublemakers as efficiently as possible, it's a major problem. Especially when everyone from the dean to the guidance counselor to the principal to the parents is able to walk away from direct responsibility and make the problem the teacher's problem. Often, I felt like a soldier dropped behind enemy lines with nothing more than orders. No weapon. No helmet. No hope of reinforcements.

The goal, of course, is to have classroom behavior issues no bigger than the usual talking, texting, and tossing of debris. That's the background noise of education and hardly an impediment to teaching and learning. In fact, as I discovered with my ninth graders, it can be the setting for magic. When a teacher can get a lesson going, get the kids—or at least most of them—reading, writing, or tying a necktie, the process can be productive for them and exhilarating for their teacher.

Voices of Teachers around the Country

Corinne Driscoll, Third Grade Teacher, Syracuse, New York

Each May, during the celebration of Teacher Appreciation Week, politicians of every stripe and school superintendents everywhere write letters and make proclamations stating how much they value the service and dedication of teachers everywhere. All of these words are empty and merely pay lip service to something these leaders do not believe. By their actions, these politicians and school leaders have made it obvious that they do not appreciate, admire, respect, or comprehend the jobs of the people who spend their days with the nation's children. Nor do they understand the first thing about the children in those classrooms.

On every occasion possible, these leaders talk about incompetent and ineffective teachers as if they are the norm instead of the rare exception. They create policies that tie teachers' hands, making it more and more difficult for them to be effective. They cut budgets, eliminate classroom positions, overload classrooms, remove supports, choose ineffective and downright useless instructional tools, set up barriers to providing academic assistance, and then very quickly stand up and point fingers at teachers, blaming them for every failure of American society and washing their own hands of any blame.

They make children endure things they would never allow for themselves: nine hours of testing over two weeks, with no breaks during each session for children as young as eight; reading tests for English as a Second Language students who have only been in the United States for one year; math tests for those same ESL students, eligible as soon as they set foot in the school; testing for children with severe learning and physical challenges. And when the scores for these children are not at the top, it's the teachers' fault.

We are taught as teachers to value the individual, that each child learns at his or her own pace, that we should vary instruction and testing to accommodate all learning styles, that all children have differing talents and all are equally valuable.

But our leaders think of children as parts on an assembly line. If we plug in A and tighten screw B, all will be well, and every child will be a carbon copy of the other—on the same date all children of the same age will get the same score on the same test.

Well, folks, education is not a product; it's a process. A school is not a factory. Children are not identical machine parts, but complex human beings coming to school with a whole variety of baggage, both good and bad. So, stop blaming the teachers and setting up roadblocks to keep us from doing what needs to be done. And keep your empty words to yourself. Your actions have already shown us what you really think.

Corinne Driscoll has been a teacher for twenty-two years in the Syracuse City School District.

THE RULES

Don't say "don't."

—Ms. P, Founding Principal, Latinate Institute

U H-OH! YOU'LL GET A U!"
     "I'm telling!"
"You'll be fired!"
"Yeah, you'll get a U for sure."

The ninth graders gleefully taunted me when I repeated what one of the students said about his homework. "I didn't know what the fuck to write," he said.

"I didn't know what the fuck to write?" I echoed in disbelief.

That the kids knew teachers were never supposed to utter "fuck" wasn't surprising. But that they knew it was an offense worthy of an Unsatisfactory rating proved just how well they knew the System. The students were quite adept at blaming a wide array of their own problems, misbehaviors, and shortcomings on bad teachers:

- "I don't come to school because I can't stand that class."
- "I didn't hand in the homework because the teacher never can explain what we're supposed to do."
- "I talk in that class because the teacher can't control the class and because everybody acts up all the time."

While this kind of blame-shifting has been going on for as long as schools have been in session, these days the kids' reports of bad teachers are given some credence since they suggest that the teacher is a rule-breaker.

In today's public schools it's easy to break the rules. There are, after all, so many rules. Choose a noun, any noun, and chances are there's a rule that goes along with it. At Latinate, Ms. P left no rules to chance, publishing them in a constantly updated cascade of photocopied decrees that came from the Department of Education as well as her own "Amazing!" leadership.

Typical of Ms. P's rules was the rubric (set of standards) for the hallway bulletin boards that teachers decorated. Here is an excerpt:

> The celebration of student achievements is a highly valued practice at Latinate. Each teacher is assigned a hallway bulletin board on a monthly or bimonthly basis. Mounting of exhibits starts on the 15th of each month, and final inspections are done by the assistant principal on the 17th of each month. Assessment rubrics for bulletin boards are found in Appendix B.

Appendix B pointed out, with a five-column rubric, the very specific requirements for "celebrating student achievement."

"Your performance on the bulletin board will be part of your professional evaluation," the assistant principal reminded us.

In other words, the path to an Unsatisfactory rating is paved with bulletin boards that display student work but do not explicitly present the New York State Learning Standard that the students are addressing with their work. Also, the grading of the student work must not be just letters (A, B, C, and so on) and certainly not just words (such as "Great," "Lovely," and "Terrific"). The grades must be expressed as specific numeric values based on a rubric for that assignment. Oh, boy.

While Ms. P set out the rules in legalistic language that was an inevitable "Gotcha!" for any teacher she was eager to build a case against, the exacting standards of the bulletin board extend— and are followed—throughout the New York City public school system. Visit a New York City school, and chances are you will find hallway bulletin boards for every grade level and every subject, all following the template.

A first-year teacher at another Bronx middle school told me how she decorated a bulletin board with the students' work jauntily hung amid bright autumn leaves, along with all of the requisite rubrics and teacher comments. But rather than set a festive fall mood, the board put her assistant principal on high alert, as though it were a terrorist threat. A memo was immediately issued cautioning the staff to never (*never!*) display student work diagonally. It must be hung straight up and down.

My buddy, Ms. Lyons, told me that administrators were so fixated on bulletin boards because inspectors from the Department of Education could turn up at any time, and that inappropriate display of outstanding student achievement could cost a school many valuable rating points. Ah, yes, the pageant. It must *look* like a successful school.

It was soon obvious that no one expected the DOE inspectors to actually *read* what was on the bulletin boards, because what I saw posted around Latinate seemed to have been selected for its visual impact, not its standing as remarkable student work. For instance, Ms. P praised a bulletin board showcasing eighth-grade research papers on French philosophers who had influenced the American Revolution.

"Amazing!" said Ms. P.

The paper that hung front and center began:

> Charles-Louis de Secondat, baron de La Brède et de Montesquieu was born at the Château de La Brède in the southwest of France. His father, Jacques de Secondat, was a soldier with a long noble ancestry. His mother, Marie Françoise de Pesnel who died when Charles de Secondat was seven, was a female inheritor of a large monetary inheritance who brought the title of barony of La Brède to the Secondat family.

And so forth for several pages, as this direct lift from Wikipedia demonstrated not scholarship, but merely the eighth grader's mastery of her computer's cut-and-paste function.

The paper's title page had a lovely screen-grab portrait of the philosopher. Unfortunately, one of the only words that the student actually typed in—Montesquieu—was misspelled.

Another "Amazing!" bulletin board was fashioned by the lead teacher, someone Ms. P often pointed to as a model for us in every way. The display showed eleventh-grade work. Her students had illustrated plot elements of Arthur Miller's profoundly important play, *The Crucible*, by drawing colorful stick figures.

Ms. P also constantly reminded us of the student non-negotiables, those rules that she expected to be accepted as readily as the Law of Gravity. She dictated that no "if," "and," or "but" could get around these immutable rules. Among them:

- Be prepared every day: Have classroom supplies, homework, and other assignments readily available.
- Do not eat food, candy, or gum outside of the lunchroom.
- Leave beepers, radios, music players, games, laser pens, and playing cards at home. *They will be confiscated.* Cell phones are allowed but must be turned off and stay in the student's locker. *If seen outside the locker, they will be confiscated.*

Despite the obvious fictional nature of these rules—students without homework, eating candy, and texting on cell phones were common around Latinate—the non-negotiables were posted throughout the school. There were few American flags and only an occasional, unframed photograph of President Barack Obama. But each classroom, displayed in gigantic, sealed-behind-acrylic printing, were the school's mission statement, core values, non-negotiables, and other propaganda, wishful thinking, window dressing, or pageantry.

As with most of the new, small public schools in New York City, Latinate was founded on the model of a charter school. Exactly what that means isn't clear. For some, it means a school run by a private corporation spending public money. For others, it's a school with hand-picked students—or at least kids whose parents want them to attend this school—as well as nonunion teachers and a long school day. But regardless of the actual setup, the designation as a charter school does give the impression that it's not education as usual. To the general public, the term "charter school" has come to mean, "Oh! *Finally*, someone knows what they are trying to do here!" Of course, that is rarely true.*

Nonetheless, charter schools seem to bolster the idea that there are straightforward answers to very complex problems. Having a charter, a mission statement, core values, and other documents with purposeful names and formal language provides a whiff of both modern corporate efficiency and the principles embodied in brief, though powerful statements such as the Declaration of Independence and the U.S. Constitution. With the ubiquitous mission statement at Latinate, we were trying to…

> [D]evelop high-achieving students of good character who use academic, technological, and social skills to inspire others, succeed in college, and accede to positions of social power that improve the community and the broader nation.

How would that be achieved? By enforcing the non-negotiables, of course. On the surface, these rules were fairly straightforward and not that difficult to follow. But even a kid who was trying to play by the rules could easily run afoul of, say, the non-negotiable that stated: "Wear full Latinate Institute uniform each day; all outer clothing must remain in closets."

As with many of New York City's charter-style schools, Latinate had a school uniform that resembled the old Catholic school outfit. The idea is to keep the kids from fussing about and being distracted by fashion. You also don't want gang colors and other partisan markers in the school. Economy, too, is used as a

---

*As pointed out earlier in this book, an often-cited 2009 study by Stanford University's Center for Research on Education Outcomes (CREDO) found "sobering" achievement levels among students at 2,403 charter schools in sixteen states. In other words, most of these kids would have performed better in a traditional public school.

selling point. As French Toast, a leading supplier of school uniforms, says on its website:

> Uniforms have a helpful leveling effect in school systems where there is economic diversity. It can be quite expensive to dress our children. $300.00 per child is not an unreasonable amount spent on each child for back-to-school wear. But that total is for September, only. Most parents continue to purchase new outfits throughout the entire school year as the weather and fashion perceptions change. That's a lot of money that can be well spent elsewhere in most households.
>
> The average expenditure for a complete French Toast uniform (pant/jumper, shirt/blouse, sweater, tie) is $45.00. Most children will require two sets of them. That's $90.00 total, period, for the year.

But for those who wanted to add to or fill out their Latinate wardrobes, options included:

Girl's Uniform

Wrap-Around Kilt: Latinate Maroon Plaid	$45
Slacks: Khaki Flat-Front, Mid-Rise	$26
Blouse: White Long-Sleeve, Button-Down Collar	$22
Sweater: Latinate Maroon w/3-Stripes, V-Neck	
w/Latinate Logo	$47
Blazer: Latinate Maroon, Polyester	$67
Tie: Maroon & Khaki Stripe w/Latinate	
Stripe and Name	$11
Knee-Highs: Latinate Maroon Opaque	$4

Tights: Latinate Maroon	$9
Headband: Latinate Maroon Plaid	$8
Belt: Black/Brown reversible	$9
Gym T-Shirt: Ash w/Latinate Logo	$11
Sweatpants: Latinate Maroon	$15

Boy's Uniform

Slacks: Khaki Poly/Cotton	$36
Shirt: White Long-Sleeve, Button-Down Collar w/Latinate Logo	$22
Tie: Maroon & Khaki Stripe w/Latinate Stripe and Name	$11
Sweater: Latinate Maroon w/3-Stripes, V-Neck w/Latinate Logo	$47
Blazer: Latinate Maroon, Polyester	$67
Socks: Black Crew	$4
Gym T-Shirt: Ash w/Latinate Logo	$11
Sweatpants: Latinate Maroon	$15

Always worn with black shoes—not sneakers. Always with the shirt tucked in. Always with the tie tied. Always without any outerwear, scarves, hats, hoodies, or other nonuniform apparel. No other T-shirt permitted in gym.

To an adult, this doesn't seem like a very difficult assignment. But for a kid coming from a chaotic life that may find him or her living with various aunts, uncles, or grandmothers at various times; who has to get up before sunrise to catch a city bus to school; and who might be powered only by the sugar-laden free breakfast offered in the cafeteria, I thought turning up in anything resembling the requisite uniform was quite impressive.

But if Ms. P saw a kid out of uniform (untied tie, sneakers, brown shoes, hoodie over the official sweater), the student *and* teacher were in big trouble. Though exactly what sort of big trouble was never quite clear to me, nor to any of my students.

The reason for this lack of clarity? Ms. P's hand-off of discipline to the classroom teachers. Of her numerous "expectations" for teachers, the most important and most troubling was:

> **The individual teacher will handle all behavior problems in the classroom.**

As I said before, the kids' classroom behavior and adherence to all rules, expectations, and non-negotiables were the teacher's problem. Whether it required conferencing with parents or lunching with the perpetrators to try to see eye to eye, the individual classroom teacher was responsible for keeping all of the students quiet, properly attired, and on task all the time. The emphasis was on *all* students and *all* the time.

Clearly, I wouldn't be meeting expectations if I called in the school aide, the large, gruff bulldog of a man who spent most of his workday watching for out-of-classroom misbehavior at the junction of Latinate's three hallways. It was even worse to require the help of the assistant dean, whose rank as a captain in the Army Reserve gave him a badass manner and reputation. The dean and assistant principal were similarly off-limits for a teacher who wanted to meet Ms. P's expectations.

Ms. P's dictate meant there was no SAVE room. An acronym for Schools Against Violence in Education, the SAVE room traditionally is where out-of-control students are sent so they don't disrupt the class.

As the veteran English teacher Ms. Patel regularly pointed out, referring to previous schools in her long and productive career, if a kid was too disruptive, the teacher would just open the classroom door and summon an assistant principal who would take the student to the SAVE room. The threat of being sent to the SAVE room usually was enough to dial down bad behavior. Outside of Ms. P's cabinet, every experienced teacher I talked to in high-needs schools said that a SAVE room, or something like it, was essential.

As noted in the previous chapter, in my time at Buchanan, I saw how the equivalent of a SAVE room had worked fairly well. It got disruptive kids out and kept potentially disruptive kids under control through the threat of being thrown out. Most important of all, it helped make a better classroom environment for the kids who really wanted to do the work or at least didn't mind doing the work. And that, by far, was the majority of kids.

But SAVE rooms are so old school. Abolishing them and not risking injury to the errant student's self-esteem is part of today's successful school. After all, how can you conduct a pageant of happy, productive scholars in a cathedral of learning if there is also a twenty-first-century dungeon where you can banish them?

Latinate, Ms. P insisted, would have no SAVE room. It was the bedrock of her educational philosophy. The *teacher* needed to handle and solve behavior issues in the classroom, even if those behavioral issues were beyond the teacher's scope of expertise or ability to handle, as many of these kids' problems were.

The notion that the classroom teacher can and should handle the vast majority of discipline issues has spread as school reform puts more power in the hands of administrators. As a result, principals and assistant principals around the country can make this rule, enforce it, and then turn a blind eye to behavior problems by just tossing them into a classroom for the teacher to figure out.

A teacher who was visiting a Bronx middle school told me a story that vividly demonstrates this abdication of responsibility and passing the buck to classroom teachers. The visiting teacher was in the assistant principal's office when a school aide brought in a sixth-grade boy who was very upset. His teacher had sent him to the assistant principal because the boy had pulled up a girl's skirt, exposing her underpants to the entire class.

"Why did you do that?" the assistant principal asked.

"It was her—she started it," the boy said. "We were playing Bangkok—and she shouldn't have been playing."

Hmm, Bangkok, the visiting teacher thought. It is so nice that these kids are playing something exotic and international—and she wondered exactly how you played.

"What's Bangkok?" the assistant principal asked.

"We play it in the cafeteria all the time," the boy said, as though he were explaining the most obvious fact. "I had a metal bat and…"

"You had a metal bat? In the cafeteria?" the assistant principal gasped.

"Yes—the principal saw me," the boy said. "The principal knew I had it."

"He can't have known you had a bat," the assistant principal said in a horrified tone, coming to the defense of his boss.

"Everyone saw it," the boy said, dismissing the concern. "Anyway, we were playing Bangkok—you know, when you go over to your friend and bang his cock really hard. So she came over and played Bangkok with me—and she hit me really hard." The boy winced. "And I told her not to do that. But she laughed."

"And so you lifted up her skirt?" the assistant principal said in a shocked tone.

"No—I pushed her—and her skirt lifted up…"

"Now, you know that you can't push other students," the assistant principal told the boy. "Remember that. And go back to class."

In other words, *I've done everything I'm going to do. Now get out of here and let your teacher deal with any further fallout from playing Bangkok.*

At Latinate, Ms. P announced this classroom-teacher-is-responsible rule at the August new-teacher orientation. I was a freshly minted pedagogue, but already I could see the problem.

"Then what leverage do we have over the kids?" I asked.

"There is a pyramid of intervention and discipline," I was told. "It is in your packet of materials."

The PID consisted of tools such as after-school detention, calls home, bad grades, parent meetings, and suspension. When I was a high school student, these were lethal weapons in a teacher's arsenal. A call home? I'd still be recovering from the punishment. But it didn't take me long to discover that many of the kids at Latinate viewed even the peak of the pyramid of intervention and discipline as little more than an inconvenience. After all, their parents—if they could be reached at all—had far bigger issues than a kid's misbehavior in class. One grandmother who came to see me about her grandson's nonstop disruptions in my eighth-grade class was trying to remember the last time she had visited the school.

"It was when Artie was killed by the cop," her grandson helpfully offered.

"Yes," she said, the timeline suddenly clear. "Fourteen months ago."

So, while the kids monitored my performance and U-caliber infractions, my real leverage with them was, well, not much of anything. Unless I could convince my students otherwise—that I *really* did have some sort of power over them—I could see this situation as a giant boulder barreling down a mountain. And it was going to roll right over me.

CLASSROOM MANAGEMENT

A nationwide study involving more than 2,300 teachers identified help with classroom management and instructional skills as their top need. Teachers wanted assistance to deal effectively with students' negative and/or disruptive behaviors.

—American Psychological Association, 2006

THESE KIDS HATE MEXICANS and they hate gays," the special-education teacher told me one day.

"It must be tough for a gay Mexican at this school," I laughed.

"Yeah," he smiled, "but I manage."

Although just three years out of college, at twenty-six, Mr. Rodriguez was already a special-ed wizard and the General Patton of the classroom.

"They think I'm a badass," he said. "Try it. Make them think you're a badass."

"'I shot a man in Reno, just to watch him die,'" I joked, reciting the line from Johnny Cash's "Folsom Prison Blues."

"Yes," the lead teacher chimed in. "Tell them that. They won't know the reference, and they'll think you're a badass."

In my tenth-grade class, Natasha and her posse clearly didn't buy into my badass act, but I nonetheless had the ninth graders under control.

"Most of them are new to the school, and they're scared. They don't act scared, but they are," Ms. Lyons, the tough-talking science teacher, told me. "You can use that to your advantage."

Every experienced teacher says that you have to show the kids who's in charge. One story goes that a teacher at a particularly tough school would start the academic year by getting the students in the room and dramatically slamming the door. He'd then tell the kids to shut up and throw a desk across the classroom for emphasis. But in reality, teachers aren't permitted to do that. Only the students can get away with throwing desks across the classroom.

"They like it when you're really mean to them," one long-time teacher told me. "They respect that."

I could be tough, but *mean*? I didn't get into this to be mean.

The administration never took sides on the tough-versus-mean controversy. Instead, the issue was cloaked in vague euphemisms for what to do. "Classroom management is very important at our school," I recalled the assistant principal telling me when he hired me.

The term "classroom management" was also tossed around a lot in my teacher-training courses. But what, exactly, does it mean?

In its simplest terms, it's keeping the kids in their seats and keeping them quiet. Kids do not do this naturally. And while some kids grasp the concept and comply after years of teachers, parents, and administrators reinforcing the message, the Latinate students were not, as a group, among them. At most, some had been conditioned to sit down and be quiet for a specific teacher at a specific time. They might do it for Ms. Lyons because "she's so grouchy." They might do it for Mr. Bookbinder "because sometimes he gets so serious." They might do it sometimes for the lead teacher "because she talks to me in a way that makes me feel really stupid if I don't do as she tells me."

But those explanations were as far as it went. From what I could see, the kids had no idea that sitting down and being quiet was a prerequisite for learning. If anyone had ever told them that, none had heard it over the din and roar of the classroom. Therefore, classroom management meant making the kids do what you want them to do for the same reason that TV's Cesar the Dog Whisperer gets the Dobermans and pit bulls to roll over and beg to have their bellies rubbed.

That reason, of course, is…well, part respect, part affection, part unwillingness to fight, part routine, part…damned if I could put my finger on it. But every teacher has tips on how to achieve it.

- Spend as much time as necessary—days, *weeks*, if necessary—explaining the rules.
- Don't let kids get up to throw things away or sharpen pencils (especially sharpen pencils!) without permission.
- Be such a hardass that the kids don't see you smile until Christmas.
- Never, ever yell.
- Acknowledge good behavior (as opposed to just the bad behavior).
- At the end of class, allow them to leave only in groups—not all at once.

Sure. Good points. But how do you implement each of these, let alone all of them at the same time, without prior practice? From what I could see, classroom management skills come with experience. Like learning how to ride a bike. There are ways to speed up the process, such as working with a veteran teacher who coaches the newcomer the way a friend might help with your tennis swing. Another way to get a head start on developing classroom management skills is to have special-education training.

That was the background of Mr. Rodriguez, who exhibited the same steady, unflinching certainty as the Dog Whisperer. As a special-ed teacher, he had more training in handling disruptive kids than a mainstream teacher. On top of it, he truly was a gifted teacher and a natural-born badass.

I tried to emulate him, but it didn't last long, since I'm not a high school Dirty Harry (as Mr. Rodriguez and most other teachers recommended I be). I'm *enthusiastic*. And it had quickly become clear to me that quality was not particularly valued at Latinate, since it didn't shut down the worst of the classroom miscreants. The result, as I mentioned earlier, was that within two weeks of the start of school, I was relieved of my duties in tenth-grade English and transferred to eighth-grade English.

Anyone who thinks that eighth graders are just elementary-school kids in a closer-to-eye-level package hasn't spent much time in a classroom. Or considered the effect of surging hormones. And those who believe that "eighth grader" and "cuddly" belong even in the same thesaurus haven't contemplated students on their second or third tour of eighth grade. There might be no human being alive with more of a "nothing to lose" attitude than an eighth grader who has repeated English twice already.

So another approach was needed—and fast. One day, I had a breakthrough. One of the biggest, meanest, and most outrageous of the permanent eighth graders at Latinate was sixteen-year-old Africah. From the start, she did what she wanted as she wanted when she wanted in my class. She was the Natasha quartet of tenth-grade girls in one kid. Early on, in the middle of my lesson, Africah noisily got up and opened a locker.

"Please close the locker and sit down, Africah," I said.

She ignored me. I repeated myself.

She continued rummaging through the locker. I could feel the eyes of the class going from her to me. Her to me.

"Please close the locker and sit down," I said, walking toward her.

She turned and snarled. "Back it up, mister. Back it up." She wanted a fight.

The eyes of the class were going back and forth as at a tennis match. I couldn't back down. But I couldn't fight, either. There was more to classroom management than just a badass attitude. And badass wasn't working here. I was on my own to come up with Plan B.

"Back it up?" I said. "Who did that song? 'You'se a big fine woman, when you back that thang up. Call me Big Daddy when you back that thang up.'"

Huge laugh. Africah and the kids suddenly started rapping Juvenile's 1999 hit:

> Girl, you workin with some ass, yeah
> You bad, yeah
> Make a nigga spend his cash, yeah
> His last, yeah...

A minute later, the locker was closed and Africah was in her seat, yelling at the other kids to "Shut the fuck up! He's trying to teach."

From then on, whenever she said, "Shut the fuck up! He's trying to teach!" I told the class, "That's why I love this woman."

With my ninth-grade classes, however, I wasn't looking to silence them. As far as I was concerned—and as far as most of my students were concerned—the writing workshop was doing just fine. Each period started with me standing by the door, welcoming the students, telling them, as Buchanan's Mr. Russo did, "Okay, let's get started. The Do Now is on the board." If today's lesson was on how to build a strong introduction for an essay, the Smart Board might glow with:

> Do Now: Write YOUR definition of "Friendship" (at least three sentences).

The Do Now also was written in marker on the whiteboard, since Ms. P refused to acknowledge digital projection as a valid way of posting the elements of the lesson that she required on display during each class. The kids would come in, jostling their way to their assigned seats, while I would turn from the door saying, "Let's go. The timer is running."

Cristofer, the self-styled Puerto Rican tough, was the official timer. Before I gave him this job, he was well known for his non-sequitur class disruptions. There was no way to know what would trigger his shouting about his favorite sports team or pretending to be an action-movie hero, but I quickly discovered that a class job kept him focused and channeled his offbeat energy.

Ms. P and the lead teacher were stopwatch fanatics when it came to monitoring the progression of a lesson, and their choreography of the classroom made it important to teach at a brisk pace. With that in mind, I bought a digital kitchen timer and gave the kids one minute to get out their homework and put away their phones. Three minutes to write the Do Now. Minutes as well as fractions of minutes to perform various tasks.

This worked far better with the ninth graders than the eighth graders, who refused to be corralled by anything as abstruse as chronometry.

"Give them three minutes for the Do Now," I'd say, and Cristofer (or the official timer in every other period) would adjust the dial and call out the time at thirty-second intervals.

"Two and a half minutes…"

"Two minutes…"

Cristofer was dependable and otherwise very well behaved. He even returned the timer to me each day as he left class. For me, Cristofer was becoming a model of good behavior. Next stop: Getting him to do his schoolwork more frequently.

"Oh, Cristofer? He's the worst. The worst!" Ms. Nenza, the fresh-out-of-school English teacher, confided. "He's in my reading class and he's uncontrollable."

I told her about the timer. But I don't think she believed me, and her problems continued.

This type of countdown would be nerve-racking to an adult, but it helped focus the kids and get them to work. During these three minutes, I'd move around the room with my clipboard, attempting to note everyone's homework while I stamped each paper with a little rubber stamp of a thumbs-up or a smiling face. Another teacher had suggested I buy a stamp, and it was a great investment. The promise of a stamp on their paper could make almost any kid sit still for a minute or two.

Attendance was taken by another student who I knew would be talking if this job hadn't been assigned. Although the rules were quite explicit about students not handling attendance, almost every teacher made that a class job. And as we moved through each part of the lesson, yet another kid crossed off the previous activity on the agenda that was posted on the back wall. The assistant principal had suggested crossing off as you go to create a sense of urgency, and he was right.

After reading the Do Now answers as well as the eighty-word essays, we moved on to vocabulary. Two other students passed out the books. Once we had spent twelve minutes reviewing "incomprehensible," "manipulate," and "maximum," two other students collected the books.

I then launched into the main lesson, based on the PowerPoints given to me by the lead teacher. We looked at how to grab the reader and present a thesis sentence. I told the kids to copy the material on the PowerPoint slides into their notebooks. Threatening to move on to the next slide made them hurry.

The assistant principal scolded me for giving the kids too much to copy, but I found that they liked doing it. It gave them a physical activity and a sense of achievement. Although copying isn't quite writing, many of my young writers saw it as such, which was a start and certainly something to work with when many of them barely had a grasp on how to write complete sentences.

Group work would be ten minutes (with the official timer calling the countdown) of pairs of kids working on thesis sentences that used their definitions of "Friendship" (from the Do Now). We then reviewed their thesis sentences, talking, laughing, and often arguing (at high decibels).

Before the period ended and the kids slammed their binders shut and scrambled out the door, I reminded them to copy the homework assignment that was on both the Smart Board and whiteboard: "Eighty words: My parents don't think I'm responsible. Agree? Disagree?"

I admit it: I didn't dismiss them in the fashion Ms. P required—one table at a time. And only infrequently did I give them an exit ticket (the written answer to a wrap-up question to see if they had absorbed what they copied into their notebooks). I figured that in-class exercises and the daily eighty words told me plenty. I also failed to note each student's individual class participation in each period, simply because I was just trying to encourage any participation, rather than mark them down for lack thereof.

Worst of all, I tolerated infractions of—even the bold flouting of—a few of Ms. P's non-negotiables. That is, during my class, there was a very good chance that some kids had checked their phones; said, "Suck my dick, nigga," to another scholar; sipped an AriZona Iced Tea; and even slipped a hoodie over the school uniform. Yes, I handed out detention to regular offenders. (Michael from my homeroom was far too chatty and liberal with hugs and high fives, and some of the repeat ninth graders refused to do much of anything.)

But with so many of the kids doing the work—and seeming to enjoy it—at least in the ninth-grade classes, I didn't have to be a hardass, and I could be my enthusiastic self. And slowly but surely, their enthusiasm and quality of work and participation began to rise. As I saw it, classroom management was finally being replaced by teaching and learning.

WHAT HAS FOUR WHEELS
AND FLIES?

The average U.S. public school teacher reported spending $356 of his or her own money on school supplies and instructional materials in the 2009–10 school year. That's more than $1.3 billion nationwide.

—National School Supply and Equipment Association

WHILE THE MOST VISIBLE, classroom management is only one of several dozen standards by which a teacher is judged and determined to be effective or not by the school administration. Punctuality is also high on the list. And that makes sense. We demand that the students be on time and that lessons begin and end with the precision of a Japanese railroad timetable. But from what I could see, coordinating locomotives and miles of track would be preferable to trying to be on time when hopping from classroom to classroom as a "traveling teacher" at Latinate.

As I previously mentioned, many of the teachers circulated among classrooms in the course of a day. After my first three periods of ninth graders, I was on the move. And the traveling wasn't as much of an issue as the timing and encumbrances that had to accompany my mortal coil from classroom to classroom.

Ms. P's expectation was—not unreasonably—that the teacher greet the students at the door and usher them into the classroom at the start of each period. But another expectation was—not unreasonably—that students never be left alone in a classroom and that a room without a teacher be emptied of kids and locked. But what happens when, say, Mr. Owens is teaching on the far reaches of one hall, and at the end of the period no teacher and students are coming into the classroom, yet Mr. Owens is required to be at the other end of the school for the start of the next period in four minutes? How does Mr. Owens get all of the students out of the room and lock the door behind him and beat his next class to the classroom while navigating the crowded hallways during the four-minute class change with his cart?

Yes, always with his cart. Just as a street sweeper has a barrel and a ragman has a wagon, a traveling teacher at Latinate had a cart. Only with less dignity attached to it. My cart was scrounged up by the school aide who was very proud of himself for being quicker than the trash collectors.

"It just needs some tightening," he said, wheeling the listing, rattling steel apparatus toward me.

The cart had started life decades before as a way to make a computer portable. This was at the dawn of the data-processing era, when processing units were the size of small refrigerators and the screens weren't much bigger than what is on today's cell phones. This meant the cart had a high shelf and two lower areas that were segmented with partitions that made about as much sense as the division of Berlin during the Cold War. Painted institutional tan, it wasn't much, but it was *mine*. I put a piece of tape on it and wrote OWENS in black Sharpie. I brought in tools from home and tightened the numerous fasteners.

Without a cart, a traveling teacher is the educational equivalent of a sideshow juggling and plate-spinning act. The books I used were typically in class sets. That is, enough copies for just one class. So if I wanted to use the vocabulary book for classes in two different classrooms, I had to haul them around with me. Paperback dictionaries and thesauruses were in similarly short supply, so I grabbed every copy I could find and built a rolling reference section.

We did, however, have hundreds of copies of *The Yearling; The 7 Habits of Highly Effective Teens; Bud, Not Buddy*; and *Maniac Magee*. As the school year started, box upon box of brand-new teen novels and nonfiction books about the Constitution, careers in science, and great African-Americans and Hispanic-Americans arrived to fill our already bulging classroom libraries.

"Classroom library is well stocked and organized thematically or by genre and is easily accessible," said one of the numerous items on the good teacher "must-do" checklist distributed at orientation. This meant that if you used a classroom any time during the day, you were responsible for making sure its library met expectations.

I worked after school to stock and thematically organize the bookshelves in both of the classrooms I used daily, but I still couldn't attract the students to them. I assigned books to the kids and gave them the chance to select their own, though they rarely used them, except as weapons of last resort when throwing stuff at each other. For a teacher who wanted to hide something, stashing it virtually anywhere in the classroom library was a safe bet.

Along with stacks of books, my cart had a small plastic bucket filled with pens and pencils. I had bought a few hundred Bic pens and scores of school-bus-yellow pencils when I saw them on sale just before the school year started. The kids never seemed to have a writing implement when they needed one. Whenever I asked my eighth-period students how they had gone through a whole school day without a pen or pencil, I'd get just an "I dunno" shrug.

I made supplying the kids a top priority, because copying material into their notebooks was part of virtually every lesson. Unless I had plenty of paper and writing implements on hand, the class would erupt into a South Bronx version of the pit at the Chicago Mercantile Exchange, but instead of traders shouting, reaching, and shoving in a frenzy of buying and selling, the students were doing all that in a frenzy to locate their missing school supplies or grab at others'.

I thought it was important to limit this clamor as much as possible, partially because bringing them back from classroom hunting and gathering took a couple of minutes, time that could have been spent filling their heads with "challenging, measurable pedagogy," or at least filling their notebooks with something that resembled schoolwork. But the most important reason to avoid this cacophony for pen and paper was that it could attract the dean or assistant principal who would charge through the door with that "*What the hell is going on here?*" look, which always helped knock me down a notch in the kids'—and administration's—estimation. Noise was indicative of poor classroom management skills. Of losing control of the situation. Of being a bad teacher.

"The teacher is the captain of the ship," Ms. P told us during orientation. "The classroom is your ship." In my eyes, that made the administration the Coast Guard. Or pirates.

A teacher I had observed at Buchanan had a clever solution to the problem of "Mister, I don't have a pen." He bought a bunch of pens and then sold them to the students for twenty-five cents each. The proceeds were used to buy more pens. The kids were so accustomed to the system that they would quietly get up during class, hand the teacher a quarter, and receive a pen. A silent, undisruptive transaction. I got the sense that the kids were more careful with these pens since they cost money that otherwise could go toward Skittles, Jolly Ranchers, or AriZona Iced Tea.

But at Latinate, such transactions were forbidden. So, instead of holding on to the pens and pencils as valuable tools, the kids typically discarded them. After class, I'd retrieve pens and pencils from the floor and put them into the plastic bucket on my cart.

The cart also had piles of worksheets, old homework, and papers that had to be handed back to students who were never there.

"Your cart's a mess," the lead teacher told me early on as I rolled past her permanent classroom with its neat, homey touches. "The kids see all those papers, and they know you're disorganized. They know they can tell you that they gave you an assignment and you lost it."

I hadn't encountered many missing-assignment con jobs, since those students who handed in their work typically did so within a week of the deadline, and those who didn't hand it in didn't even go to the trouble of lying. Still, I took her criticism to heart and worked on organization, printing class rosters and grade sheets late into the night and snapping them into period-specific clipboards that were boldly labeled and arranged as neatly as possible on my cart. It was still an overwhelming amount of data for me to record, even in tidy rows and columns, as I roamed the classroom stamping homework and quelling disturbances. To the students, what mattered was that I had a clipboard and it looked like I was keeping score.

Every now and then, an otherwise good, cooperative student who had recently ingested a fistful of candy would start throwing papers or yelling at another kid. I just stood silently looking at the misbehavior and then raised my clipboard and pretended to take notes.

"*What are you doing?*" the offender would ask.

"Making a note of your behavior," I would say as stonily as possible, without looking up.

Usually, the student would settle down. Others, especially those eighth graders with longstanding behavior issues, weren't about to let a clipboard—or anything else I could think of—keep them from shouting, pounding, or rapping.

A plastic cup held my markers. Not just the markers I used to write the Ms. P-required lesson details, but also the marker I gave to a student to cross off each item on the agenda as we went through it. I quickly learned that in some classes—especially the eighth-grade classes—I couldn't hand a marker to just *any* student, since crossing items off the agenda inevitably led to drawing penises on the whiteboard.

Anyone who has been in the educational system for more than fifteen minutes knows that "erasable" is the key word when selecting a marker for use on the whiteboard. An eraser that's very similar to an old-fashioned chalk eraser does a good job of smearing the ink sufficiently so you can write in that spot again. To get the board residue-free, just wipe it down with a damp cloth (which I did daily).

But use a Sharpie, and you suddenly have a visceral understanding of the word "permanent." You can wipe. You can wash. But you will still see whatever you wrote on the board as a background motif. Plus, every other teacher who ever uses this classroom will know you are an idiot, incapable of distinguishing between markers. Take it from a permanent-marker idiot.

I was determined to make up for my whiteboard inadequacies

with Smart Board wizardry. Basically a digital projector that's connected to a computer that provides not only access to the Internet but also to all sorts of clever software, the Smart Board is a giant touch screen that makes education fun, engaging, and very high tech. The screen measures nearly five feet wide and four feet high. You can see it even with the classroom lights on. It's billed as a technological adjunct to the teacher. But in fact, many school administrators see it as a way to ensure vibrant, interactive, and engaging lessons despite the presence of lazy bad teachers.

With that in mind, the $7,000-plus cost is easy to justify. Funding often comes from private foundations and school-reform organizations that provide seed money for charter and charter-style schools. That's how Latinate got Smart Boards installed in most of its classrooms. However, the money for this sort of whizbang seems to dry up once the wires are run and the school is open.

These Smart Boards were state-of-the-art when Latinate was founded six years earlier. Now, of course, they were neither well maintained nor in much of a state of operation. Getting the board to fire up and display what it was supposed to always brought me a measure of delight and relief that proved the existence of a deity. And getting it to work consistently required a remote control.

"Smart Boards do not need a remote control," the lead teacher insisted when I asked for one after a big rectangular box with an error message appeared on the board and wouldn't go away.

"No," she said flatly, making a Ms. P-caliber "How many times do I have to tell you not to waste the administration's time?" facial expression. "You *don't* need a remote control for the Smart Board."

But from my days at *Popular Photography* magazine when I used a very similar type of technology, I knew that the type of Canon projector at the heart of the Smart Board resets only with its remote control. So I prowled the school and beseeched the school aide for remote controls of any sort that could be found. After a couple of weeks of having the kids copy around the big rectangular error box on the Smart Board, I turned up a remote that worked. Sure enough, it was the only way to get that box to disappear.

"There's a big rectangular box with an error message on the Smart Board in my room," Ms. Lyons said one day, tech-phobic panic in her voice as she hurried from her room across the hall. "Even the kids don't know how to get it to go away."

"Ahh," I said, going to the cart for my battery-powered magic wand. "Allow me." For once in this place, I felt needed and useful.

The computers that were attached to the Smart Boards, however, were in much worse shape. With any of these vintage Dells (circa 2004), there was an excellent chance that the kids had rigged it so that busty, middle-finger-shooting rapper and pop star Nicki Minaj was the default image on the screen. Plus, the computers were so loaded with viruses that the processors moved no faster than my cart through the hallways at class change. But if I suggested that the kids were screwing with a computer, my superiors waved me off like the madman I was. "The computers are password protected," I was told.

"What's the password for the computer?" I asked an eighth-grade class one day.

"Delladmin1," they sang in unison. I knew that a full-blown Nicki Minaj Smart Board attack wasn't far in the future.

"You know, the kids know the password on the classroom computers," I told the lead teacher.

"Well, they shouldn't be getting anywhere near the computer in your classroom anyway," she responded curtly, which I read as suggesting that computer problems were a byproduct of poor classroom management skills. Though I hadn't observed any students near the computers in my classes, I still made a mental note to add that to my list of things to manage while teaching.

Teachers at Latinate weren't required to bring their own computers, but many did. To be sure that I could get my classes under way with a minimum of technical interruptions—because I knew that the second I was more focused on electronics than the kids, projectiles would be flying and cell phones would be buzzing—and to ensure that the PowerPoints that I had so diligently prepared the night before got a proper airing, I bought my own computer. I spent $860 for the laptop using the Department of Education discount. But almost immediately after I placed the order, I saw the identical computer on sale at Staples for $35 less than I had paid. So much for teacher discounts.

My laptop sat front and center on my cart, not just so I could keep an eye on it, but also so it could swing into action like a digitally enabled Minuteman. The power cord was ready to go into the wall, and its ports ready to receive the cables that I unhooked from the old classroom computer. If all went well—and sometimes it did—I could have the Do Now glowing in PowerPoint glory on the Smart Board as the eighth graders entered class.

But as I mentioned earlier, even then, per Ms. P, the full, neatly printed, totally detailed blackboard configuration (everything from the New York State standards addressed in today's lesson to tonight's homework) had to be on the whiteboard. And if I couldn't get it written on the board before class started, I resorted to using the traveling-teacher approach of writing it on a poster-sized sheet of paper and draping it over my cart like the huge piece of cloth covering the grand prize on a TV game show. Or like a sheet over a body on its way to the morgue.

As one period ended and my next was to begin, I typically

had to roll my cart from one end of the Latinate hallways to the other. End to end, it was no more than 400 feet. But when clogged with kids and other cart-encumbered traveling teachers, it was a long, difficult journey that took at least the full four minutes we had between classes. This building was, after all, built in the 1950s as an elementary school. The hallways were far too narrow for hundreds of backpack-wielding, McDonald's-fed high school students who believed that life is a contact sport.

"Gimme a hug," a boy would say to a girl who had been separated from him for forty-six minutes.*

"I got your hat," one boy would yell to another, darting down the clogged hallway.

"Hey, no running," shouted the school aide uselessly. "And no hats."

As I slowly pushed my cart up the hall, kids would pretend to take things off it. Kids would not notice me and bump into it. Kids would run past with their backpacks flying and catch my poster paper, dragging it onto the floor or sending it into full flight, a giant insect that was inevitably swatted down and stomped on.

"Oh, I'm sorry, mister." Big laugh.

According to the students of Latinate, my cart-driving skills were totally inadequate as I regularly tried to go faster than the

---

*As the *Today* show put it in a 2009 televised report, "High school hugging has turned into a cultural phenomenon, studied by sociologists and written about in the *New York Times*." In schools, widespread hugging can, at best, be a time-wasting hallway-snarler; at worst, it can become aggressive physical contact and harassment. As a result, teen embraces have become a regulated activity. In March 2012, it made the national news when the principal at Cliffwood, New Jersey's 900-student Matawan Aberdeen Middle School declared it a "no hugging" campus. Other schools have joined the ban, while at least one New York City school permits lunch-period-only hugs.

flow of traffic to get to my classroom before my students and occasionally collided with their butts.

"Damn! Watch where you're going, mister!"

Or much more painfully collided with the back of their ankles, which elicited the stronger: "*Damn!* Watch where you're goin', muthafucka!"

I always apologized profusely. Not because I minded trading "mister" for "muthafucka," but because I couldn't be late for class. And once I got to the classroom, it was essential—not important or high-priority, but *essential*—that I have my keys. A teacher needs keys. There is no teaching without keys.

The first key of the day opened the back door of the school so I could get in without ringing the bell that sounded so much like the fire alarm that the first dozen times I heard it, I instantly prepared to evacuate. The key also kept me from standing outside in the early morning dark, pounding on the steel door, and rousing the custodian or security guards who kept asking, "Why didn't they give you a key?"

Of course, getting "them" to give me a key wasn't as easy as it sounds. It required paperwork—a form from the school secretary on the second floor that was filled out and taken to the principal's secretary on the third floor. But the principal's secretary was so busy typing up edicts, rubrics, and assessments emanating from her boss that the form didn't make its way to the principal for quite some time. And the principal let my key request age, clearly sending me the message that her time was occupied with much more vital educational matters than whether I should receive a back-door key.

Once it was signed, I had to retrieve the form from the principal's secretary and take it to the custodian, who hurried to his key closet and made me a duplicate from the lock's master key. I was impressed by his speed, considering the custodians have problems of their own to manage. Although the teachers were required to clean up each classroom at the end of each period, the custodians nonetheless faced plenty of discarded candy wrappers and stray hair extensions under the radiators, as well as peeling paint.

Then there were, of course, classroom keys. When a classroom wasn't in use, it was locked. Otherwise, kids disappeared into it when they were supposed to be in, well, *class.* Also, unless the classroom was locked, anything except desks and books disappeared, the remnants lavishly decorated with penises and other paraphernalia.

Although I used only two classrooms on a typical day, I rarely had the right keys. Room assignments were so frequently changed—as were the locks themselves—that I was constantly at the mercy of the school aide, whose two rings of keys were so densely packed that it looked like he was carrying brass pinecones.

"Hello, sir, could you please let us into this classroom?" I'd ask hopefully amid the roar of the period change as the eighth graders piled up in the hall around the door.

"Okay, Mr. Owens. But I have to do something for Ms. P first," he'd say, scurrying off.

By the time he returned and tried one key after another—and then one ring of keys after another—the kids were hitting each other with their backpacks, having second thoughts about attending class, and asking me, "Why didn't they give you a key?"

When the door finally flung open, I would hand the large sheet of poster paper with the details of today's lesson and the other Ms. P–required material to one of the kids and ask that it be hung on the whiteboard in the front of the room. It didn't take me long to realize that I could never give a kid a roll of tape and say, "Just tear off a couple of pieces and hang the poster." No. The poster would get hung, but in the next several seconds, the roll of tape would disappear into a crush of eighth graders and one of the smaller, weaker students would have his mouth bound like a kidnap victim. Instead, I provided two pre-torn pieces of tape. The tape, incidentally, was purchased out of my lavish teacher pay.

Mr. Bookbinder, the talkative veteran English teacher, used his lavish teacher pay to buy a poster-sized erasable whiteboard and tried using that instead of the bulky paper. I liked the idea and also bought one. It worked so much better. Easier to write on, easier to carry from classroom to classroom, and easier to display—no tape required, just rest it in the marker tray on the classroom's whiteboard. Overall, better and more dignified.

But one day, we were told that they were not acceptable, without further explanation. And we immediately stopped using the portable whiteboards.

The other essential keys were to my lockers. With steel lockers lining one wall of every classroom at Latinate, even after each student claimed one, there were plenty of lockers for teachers to use. But to store anything other than books, you needed a lock.

"Don't use a combination lock," Ms. Lyons, the South Bronx-hardened science teacher, told me. "The kids watch you open it, and they have the combination. Always use a key lock. A good one."

That meant one that's hard to pick. Because over the course of a forty-six-minute period, a paper clip can do wonders to the innards of anything but the most hard-core lock. For those of us who stored our car keys, cell phone, wallet, and lunch in the locker, this meant Diebold, Fort Knox, atomic-attack-proof security. When one of my students noticed that I kept cans of Diet Dr. Pepper in one of my lockers, I sensed safe-cracking moving up on his list of potential career paths. If he had known I also had several packs of

Trident sugar-free bubble gum in there, I could have expected to soon hear a drilling sound, followed by a small explosion.

The first week of school, a brand-new music teacher had her car keys and cell phone disappear. She quit on the spot and got a ride home.

"I worked with a teacher who put everything he had in one of those little fanny packs and then wore it right here," Ms. Lyons said, pointing to her sternum. "The kids will steal anything and everything."

Not entirely true. They would not steal books. Nor notebook paper. And not pens and pencils. Seemingly nothing to help them further their learning. Markers, on the other hand, always disappeared as seamlessly as a magician's assistant, presumably because they were so suitable for drawing genitalia in vacant classrooms.

In addition to a couple dozen markers, I lost only some soda, a couple of piles of Post-its, a thumb drive, a timer, a clipboard, and several items that resembled food. Keeping my Tic Tacs out of the kids' hands was the stuff of an action-adventure movie, with ingenious plots, stealthy raids, and daring dives over desks by both parties. I lost very little, though I was careful to the point of crazy. My laptop computer was rarely out of my hand and never out of my sight. Of course, I didn't want it to go missing, but I also knew that if it vanished, there would be no sympathy.

"Well, you shouldn't have given them the chance."

Granted, most of the kids were good kids. But that was not enough to prevent larceny from being a constant threat.

"Even the good kids will steal," Ms. Lyons told me solemnly. "Really, even the good kids."

Some kids stole for need. Some for sport. Some for pathological compulsions. So ultimately, no teacher could take any chances with the keys.

Just drop them in your pocket? Don't be an idiot. Do you wave a cape at a bull? Do you throw an empty Jack Daniels bottle out the window when driving past a cop?

A tough-talking social studies teacher with large biceps was the only one in our school who wore his keys on his belt, attached to a retracting reel, custodian-style. I knew that I lacked the lightning-quick reflexes that would be required to keep my keys hanging off my belt at desk level as I walked through a classroom of constantly moving, jumping, and jostling kids. Forbidden fruit? Hell, I'd be an easy mark. So, like everyone else, I wore them on a lanyard around my neck.

Most of us at Latinate were never issued a New York City Department of Education ID card. I could have gotten one if I'd just added a digital photo of myself to my official file with the DOE. My fingerprints were already on file (a condition of employment) and I had a note from Ms. P saying I was an employee, but by the time I found out about the photo requirement, the school year had already started, and like most teachers at the school, I was so busy getting my pedagogical house in order that I never took it any further.

So, aside from my voluminous personnel file of bad teaching, I had no official proof of my DOE existence. But with my lanyard, everyone knew I was a teacher. And where. During our just-hired orientation, Ms. P had bestowed a Latinate lanyard on each of us. A nylon ribbon in school colors with "Latinate Institute" printed in a repeating pattern, the lanyard had a ring at the end to hold the keys and a plastic buckle on the back.

"Go ahead, tug it," Ms. Lyons said to me in a double-dare tone. I pulled the lanyard.

"See, the buckle came undone," she smiled. "It has to. Otherwise, kids could strangle you."

"They would?" I asked incredulously.

"Well, they *could*."

"Hmmm," I said thoughtfully. "In that case, not only would I be dead, but the kids would have my keys."

"That's right," Ms. Lyons responded. "And you can't let the kids get your keys."

Every kid knew that the keys were the Holy Grail of school mischief, but with them hanging from the teacher's neck, snatching them—even with the strangle-proof plastic snap—would require a move a bit too close to the legal definition of assault. Even the most daring, outrageous kids knew it wasn't worth the trouble that an assault arrest would bring.

As the keys, cart, computer, and Smart Board remote control prove, logistics and equipment can have a huge impact on a teacher's performance. In fact, they can spell the difference between success and failure. The profession brings with it very specific gear and security requirements, and just getting to the classroom and getting the lesson under way always struck me as a bizarre riff on marching an army and opening a circus.

Unless the maneuvers are well organized and precisely timed, you will be late for class, and the kids, seeing you unprepared, will go wild. Yet getting the marching and material right isn't enough. The teacher also must present such a strong presence that in an instant schoolwork becomes the students' center of attention.

For traveling teachers everywhere, there is so much more than just markers and attendance sheets riding on those carts.

NOT HIGH SCHOOL AS YOU REMEMBER IT

In 2010, the five biggest donors to K–12 education were:

Bill & Melinda Gates Foundation, $209 million

Walton Family Foundation, $110 million

W.K. Kellogg Foundation, $58 million

Michael & Susan Dell Foundation, $55 million

Silicon Valley Community Foundation, $35 million

—The Foundation Center

WHAT WASN'T LOCKED AWAY from the students simply wasn't available to them at all. As one of the new small schools, Latinate didn't have much in the way of facilities.

The other high school in the building, which had nearly 100 more students than Latinate's 350, occupied the first and nearly all of the second floor of the building. It was always referred to as the "blue school" (their school color) while Latinate was "the red school." Like Latinate, it was open to all comers. But the blue school had so many applicants that each entering ninth-grade class was chosen by a lottery, resulting in a mix of students working above, at, and below grade level.

As mentioned, Latinate didn't receive a surfeit of applicants and had what amounted to open enrollment. In addition, Ms. P was always eager to take on hard cases—especially kids with behavior problems—to prove the transformational magic of her great ideas. As a result, the blue school was seen as a bunch of pampered elitists. There was virtually no contact between the two schools—faculty and students included.

"Teaching the kids in our school is much more difficult and much more important," said Mr. Bookbinder, my serially Unsatisfactory English department colleague. "Teaching in a school like the blue school is easy."

"Just look at the students downstairs," the assistant principal said. "They don't look like our students. You can tell the difference."

He was right. The difference was apparent. But it wasn't a matter of remarkably different demographics. Unlike Latinate, the blue school did have a couple of white kids (just a couple) and perhaps two dozen Asian kids among the overwhelmingly black and Hispanic student body. According to the DOE, more than 85 percent of the students at both schools qualified for free or reduced-price lunch. From what I could see, the major difference was that the blue school kids were having an experience much closer to what Americans have come to think of as "high school." And perhaps as a result, they were not only far better behaved, but also giving their school an impressive reputation for academics.

At 2:50 each day as classes ended, Latinate's dean, assistant dean, school aide, and the phys-ed teacher swept through the halls and herded the students down the stairs and out onto the sidewalk like an tsunami of adolescents. We teachers were instructed to stand by our classroom doors and usher the kids out while wishing them a pleasant evening. After the Latinate kids were shooed out, the dean and her posse followed them to the sidewalk and tried to scatter the students to keep them from bunching up and fighting.

But a kid who was late leaving the school would almost invariably be gathering books and jacket out of the locker to the sound of drums and electric guitars from the blue school.

"Why can't we have a band?" was the inevitable question.

Latinate had a music department. It consisted of a boom box carried by a teacher and a variety of drums and beaded African gourds that were locked in a basement closet next to the teachers' restroom. Occasionally the drums and gourds were hauled up the four flights of stairs to a class.

The auditorium had an upright piano on the stage, but like everything else in the building that was worth having, it didn't belong to Latinate. The piano was shared between the schools. And the blue school always seemed to have a rehearsal for a play or a music class that involved the kids standing in a circle and singing individually. Latinate used the auditorium mostly for grade-level assemblies that featured Ms. P explaining to the students how they could earn valuable prizes by demonstrating the school's core values on a daily basis.

While she spoke about academic excellence, community citizenship, reflective living, compassion, and such, we teachers walked slowly up and down the aisles and behind the students' seats *shhh*ing and scowling like a weird combination of movie-theater ushers and stalag guards. If Ms. P had to pause due to a student interruption, the teacher of the offenders received a glower before she resumed addressing the wayward scholars.

"I. Am. Speaking," Ms. P admonished, saying each word as a separate sentence. "One voice."

Compared to Ms. P, the principal at the blue school was doing a much more convincing job of being a visionary leader and pulling off the pageant of today's successful school. He was, after all, quite good at getting grants for improvements to the school and its programs.* He told one reporter that he generated $500,000 a year from outside sources.

The blue school's principal was the face of the school, the embodiment of its purpose and success, and his visage was so prominent in media reports about the school that it was as though he were the school's crest, mascot, and idol all in one. Read the blue school's promotional material, as well as news articles and videos, and you'd get the idea that this principal had leadership magic that fell like educationally enchanted pixie dust on those around him. Perhaps. But I try to avoid seeing messiahs around

---

*Grants have become an important part of funding America's public schools. Principals, teachers, and even parents increasingly apply for any of thousands of grants from government and private sources that go toward specific projects or facilities. Among those offering money to public schools are Samsung, Walmart, MetLife, and Captain Planet Foundation (yes, there is such a thing). The grants can be earmarked for anything from technology to obscure sports.

The NEA Foundation (NEAfoundation.org) offers grants as well as resource partners that include Bank of America and Nickelodeon. Other sites, including GrantsAlert.com and GrantWrangler.com, list hundreds of offerings. A web search of "grants for teachers" also will lead to the corporate sites of companies such as State Farm, Target, and Dell.

At the same time, grassroots efforts have tried to fill funding gaps. As Jean Hopfensperger reported in the Minneapolis *Star Tribune* in 2012, "About 700 million—yes, million—box tops poured into a General Mills processing center this school year, marking record-high participation in Box Tops for Education, a school fundraiser that has exploded to become the biggest in the nation…School payouts zoomed from $33 million to $74 million in just the past five years."

every corner. Especially after it turned out that Eileen, the principal of the highly rated and widely celebrated Bronx school I call the High School for Artistic Trades, was charged with manipulating data and student transcripts.

While the blue school's principal may indeed be a wonderful, gifted, transformational visionary leader, setting up an educational system that is based on every school having a transformational visionary leader like him is impossible, if not delusional. In any case, I noticed that as with Latinate, many of the blue school's teachers were also newbies, suggesting turnover that was the result of either bad teachers being booted or good teachers finding the pixie dust not quite so enchanting.

That said, the blue school principal deserved credit for getting his school a library. Latinate only had the books piled in the back of each room, the classroom library. Early in the school year, each of Latinate's English classes had an appointment to visit the blue school's library. Set on the second floor behind glass windows, it was a brand-new, high-tech oasis financed by grants. It was gorgeous. Stack after stack of books, a line of brand-new computers along the wall. Carpet. Tables. Comfortable chairs.

I led my eighth graders through, and they were dumbstruck. Even the most outrageous of them walked gently and touched nothing, knowing that this was a very special place.*

"You will be able to use this library two days a week during certain hours," Ms. Page, Latinate's librarian, told the children. "We still have to arrange the schedule with the blue school."

---

*A school without its own library is not uncommon these days in American education. A crowd-sourced Google Map, "A Nation without School Libraries," is dense with placemarks, listing hundreds of schools—and school districts—without libraries or librarians. (http://maps.google.com/maps/ms?ie=UTF8& oe=UTF8&msa=0&msid=218097749875920684270.000482bb91ce51be5802b)

The schedule wasn't ironed out for several months, and in that time, the blue school had the library to itself. Latinate, however, had Ms. Page, its very own librarian. A slight woman with a soft Caribbean accent, Ms. Page had, like Ms. Patel, been thrust upon Latinate, and Ms. P did not seem pleased with this highly paid budget-eater. Ms. Page had spent more than twenty years as a librarian in a large high school, but when it closed to make way for several new, small schools, she was tossed out, landing at Latinate. As a librarian without a library, she prepared a library-oriented bulletin board and was used as an administration utility player, spending most of her day backing up the dean, assistant dean, and school aide in monitoring the halls and making sure that the restrooms were locked during odd-numbered periods.

Three floors below, the building's gymnasium was an old-fashioned, public-school gym with a high ceiling, mesh-covered windows, a newly refinished shiny maple floor, basketball back-boards at each end, and racks holding balls of various sorts. It was shared with the blue school.

"They have gym only two days a week," Robert Johnson's mom told me when I called her in to discuss why Robert and other eighth graders were tossing each other across the desks in my eighth-period English class. "They have no way to burn off their energy."

In the winter, there was after-school basketball in the gym, and in the spring, baseball in a local park. Once the school year was well under way, Mr. Rodriguez, the special-education teacher, got a grant to start an archery program. After much fanfare and teacher recommendations as to which students could be trusted with powerfully propelled sharp objects, Mr. Rodriguez had a dozen ninth graders spread out in the cafeteria after school shooting at 40-inch bull's-eyes set up at the far end of the tables. What had been the asphalt playground when the building housed an elementary school was now the parking lot for the staffs of both Latinate and the blue school.

"I came here because they said they had fencing," Mark, the tall, studious, all-American boy, told me one day in a "Damn, I've been ripped off" tone. It was clear that he had had visions of wielding a saber, shouting "*Touché!*" and using it as a ticket out of the South Bronx and into a college with ivy on the walls. Obviously, Mark had been taken in by the six-year-old promotional brochure that trumpeted this institute and its college-bound mission. With Latinate touting highfalutin flourishes—"Fencing... School Uniforms...Advanced Placement...Individual College Planning"—it was as though Ms. P had placed Harry Potter's Hogwarts School of Witchcraft and Wizardry on city bus lines.

To many kids and their parents, the founding principal's spiel may have sounded good, though year after year, the execution was anything but. She got away with it, no doubt, because what matters to the city's Department of Education is data—grades, graduation rates, and standardized tests. Under Ms. P's leadership, those numbers seemed adequate. Fulfilling long-promised frills like art appreciation and filmmaking? If it isn't on a spreadsheet, it isn't on the DOE's radar.

"There's no fencing," said Mark, punching the air in disgust. "There aren't even any water fountains."

Well, there *were* water fountains, if you counted the liquid that bubbled from the classroom sinks. But Mark, having been duped about Latinate's fencing program, wasn't about to take any chances slurping from the fifty-five-year-old plumbing.

Like Mark, I would have welcomed a reliable flow of cold water. He was constantly thirsty, and so was I. It was as though we spent our days in a sweltering linoleum desert.

"The schools are always hot," the assistant principal told me. "It's because the students are used to a lot of heat. Especially those who live in the Projects. They keep the temperature very high in the Projects."

No matter what the temperature outside, my homeroom was stifling. Some classrooms had home-style room air conditioners stuffed into a window. But not my homeroom. And anyway, with the compressor running and the fan blowing, an air conditioner usually created too much noise for me to hear a student's question or for the students to hear me. So I found an old floor fan that had a broken stand and duct-taped it into utility. The ambient temperature was still around eighty, though with a balmy breeze.

I sweated, yet the kids—dressed in their school-uniform sweaters or blazers—complained they were cold.

"Can I get a jacket out of my locker?" one student after another asked, arms folded over their chests in a shivering gesture.

"No. A jacket is not part of the uniform," I reminded them.

"But I'm cold."

"No," I said, wiping sweat off my forehead. "If the school aide or the assistant dean comes in, you'll get detention for being out of uniform."

"But if I catch a cold, I won't be able to come to school."

Inevitably, the mention of a cold led to fake coughing, fake sneezing, fake "God bless yous," and lots of talk about snot. With that, we could get back to work until some other students remembered they were cold.

The kids' complaints and efforts to pull the lesson off track reminded me of my own high school days. But the experience I had outside the classroom so long ago at my suburban New York public school was far different from what Latinate's students were facing.

Today, so much of what Americans have long taken for granted as the typical high school experience is increasingly rare. Especially among the various institutes, academies, and centers opened under the banner of school reform and driven by student achievement. Charter-style schools that offer little more than just academics are no longer outliers. Throughout the country, as budgets shrink and data becomes more important, much that is not strictly academic and quantifiable is cut.

Each year, more and more school districts nationwide trim the "fat," programs that enrich students' lives culturally and help them grow and develop as people, but that aren't specifically academic. As a result, sports, band, art, putting on a play—even a school library—have become extras that are not taxpayer supported. Once, students held bake sales and car washes to fund activities above and beyond the basic.

Today, their principals, teachers, and parents have been forced to assume that role on a grand scale to pay for books, athletic equipment, after-school activities…in fact, just about everything. Instead of cupcakes and soapsuds, these fundraisers use the current equivalent of the hat in hand—the grant application—to beg foundations and corporations to underwrite what, until recently, most Americans would have considered the birthright of students in our public schools.

TEACHING, STEP BY STEP

A greater power than we can contradict
Hath thwarted our intents.

—William Shakespeare, *Romeo and Juliet*

WHAT LATINATE LACKED IN facilities it made up for in structure, rules, and Ms. P's expectations.

For example, Ms. P's blackboard configuration deemed that there had to be specific material on the board before class could begin. It is not uncommon in schools everywhere these days to require posting what will be covered and bulleting the objectives of the lesson. As I mentioned earlier, that's the material I had written on large, poster-sized paper and carried on my cart to each classroom.

Say, for instance, you were teaching *Romeo and Juliet* to ninth graders. One day's lesson might be examining Shakespeare's use of figurative language in an early part of the play. The learning objective might be that, at the end of the lesson, students will be able to recount and explain the use of figurative language in the first meeting of *Romeo and Juliet*.

The idea is to articulate to the students, to anyone watching, and, as a teacher, to *yourself*, exactly what you're trying to do with today's lesson. By the end of the lesson, "Students Will Be Able To" (the SWBAT you often see on school blackboards) "know," "understand," "apply," "analyze," "synthesize," or "evaluate" something. The verb you pick for the SWBAT (pronounced "swabot") is based on Bloom's Taxonomy.

Named for a 1950s-era educator, Bloom's classifies the levels of intellectual behavior involved in learning. The lowest rung is knowledge—simply knowing, naming, memorizing, stating, and so on. Understanding is next up, followed by application, analysis, and synthesis. At the very top of the scale is evaluation. For that kind of lesson, the SWBAT would use words such as "appraise," "argue," "assess," "judge," "predict," or "compare" various things to describe the students' comprehension of the lesson. In other words, at "evaluate," the kids really have mastered the material.

So, as a teacher, you have the goal to move the kids up the Bloom's scale—not just to know the figurative language in *Romeo and Juliet*, but ultimately, to be able to compare or connect it to figurative language elsewhere in the play or elsewhere in Shakespeare or in other literary works. On a good day, I could get to the second level (recount and explain) with my ninth graders. On a good day, the eighth graders would sit down (which, apparently, Bloom didn't even consider an option).

Having the SWBAT on the board is good self-discipline for a teacher. But Ms. P demanded more. Much more with her blackboard configuration, or BBC. "The purpose of the BBC is to help teachers plan and implement a coherent lesson with a beginning, middle, and end. It helps both teachers and students stay on task. By using it each day, it helps organize students and provides clear expectations," said the handout from Ms. P.

There had to be five columns—Do Now, Learning Objectives,

State Standards, Homework, Today's Agenda—and what went in each column was very specific. In theory, all good ideas, but the strictness with which Ms. P demanded that we unfailingly, religiously, precisely follow it was intimidating.

"I will not have it any other way," she said at the orientation in a stern, "don't question this" tone.

"It *must* be done that way," the lead teacher reminded me just moments before my first class. "Ms. P will have it no other way."

Getting caught in change-of-period congestion and being unable to post the BBC before the students entered the classroom wasn't an excuse. Neither was a fire drill. Nor lack of poster paper. Nor absence of tape. Nor a dried-out marker. Nor lack of time. Being a minute late with putting it up, or taking it down a minute before the end of class, was an unforgivable offense. If Ms. P caught you in any of these transgressions, she could have given Old Testament prophets a lesson in wrath. Her eyebrows instantly expressed her disapproval by resembling a pair of down escalators, and her mouth tightened, as though she were about to spit a bullet or, worse, an Unsatisfactory rating.

The material that was on the BBC had to be entered into a computer program that held our curriculum maps—exactly what we would be doing on each day of the school year and how it met specific state standards. And the BBC had to include the state standards addressed with each lesson. For instance, the New York State standards for eighth grade writing start off like this:

1. Write arguments to support claims with clear reasons and relevant evidence.
    a. Introduce claim(s), acknowledge and distinguish the claim(s) from alternate or opposing claims, and organize the reasons and evidence logically.

b. Support claim(s) with logical reasoning and relevant evidence, using accurate, credible sources and demonstrating an understanding of the topic or text.

c. Use words, phrases, and clauses to create cohesion and clarify the relationships among claim(s), counterclaims, reasons, and evidence.

d. Establish and maintain a formal style.

e. Provide a concluding statement or section that follows from and supports the argument presented.

The state standards go on like this for pages and pages and pages. So, if today's lesson was on writing an essay about *Romeo and Juliet* and using evidence and quotations to prove your point, my BBC (and curriculum map) would say under "Standards": "2 b. Develop the topic with relevant, well-chosen facts, definitions, concrete details, quotations, or other information and examples." (Not the sort of language that immediately connects with any eighth graders I have ever met.)

All of this information—in precisely the five-column (not five-row) format—had to be on the board in blue or black ink before any students entered the classroom. A teacher with neat, bold handwriting could fit this material into about six square feet of whiteboard space. And it had to be in large enough type to be visible from anywhere in the room. And all of it had to be posted for the entire period.

Teachers who didn't have a class immediately before their next class were expected to get into the classroom toward the end of the prior period and write the BBC on the whiteboard. But if there was already a class in the room during that time, it was very distracting for another teacher to come in and take over a big hunk of the board. Also, if the teacher whose class was in session had filled the whiteboard, where would the interloper's BBC go? Remember, Ms. P's rules were quite explicit: the other teacher's BBC could not be erased before the bell.

Also, I knew that I didn't like it when other teachers slipped into the classroom while I was trying to wrangle a bunch of eighth graders with just a few minutes left in class. And other teachers hated it, too, but tolerated it. One tenured, long-time science teacher, however, didn't. Ms. Adebayo—a large, fiftyish woman with a raft of degrees including a Juris Doctor from her native Nigeria, and a generally annoyed manner—scowled at me the first time I slipped into her class. The second time, immediately at the end of the period, she thrust her face into mine and said, "Stop interrupting my class."

"But Ms. P…"

"I don't care about Ms. P," Ms. Adebayo said angrily, reflecting her widely known animosity for the principal and the Unsatisfactory ratings Ms. P had bestowed on her. "Mr. Owens, stop interrupting my class."

"Got it."

Ms. P, however, told us in staff meetings that a good teacher would have the students so engaged in their rich, challenging pedagogy that another teacher at the board wouldn't be a distraction. Clearly, only bad teachers would have such concerns.

The blackboard configuration outlined the workshop model of instruction. We are living in the age of student-centric cooperative learning, and the workshop model is all about that. Basically, it provides the students with a very specific skill that they immediately practice and put to use. Such as recognizing figurative language— for instance, similes and metaphors—in *Romeo and Juliet*. Like posting the SWBAT, the workshop model is widely used today. It is *the* instructional approach in New York City public schools.

I found it a good template for lessons, though teaming the kids up rarely produced cooperative learning. My experience was that they achieved more when working by themselves. For easily distracted students, a partner to talk to, tease, or annoy is much more attractive than classwork. I also found that the way the workshop model was employed at Latinate was quite constrictive. What was a good template became a straitjacket for the instructional process. Each segment was to be precisely timed, and the pacing was to be the same in each lesson.

Although the workshop model is the standard in the New York City system, the first I heard of it was when I was hired at Latinate. And I was woefully unprepared for the precise instructional choreography it required. During my studies at Empire State College, I reviewed and produced various lesson plans. But they were of a general format, with the content and activities determining the timing and pacing. The potato chip–rating Citizen Journalism lesson that earned me an A at ESC would require a complete overhaul to be acceptable at Latinate. Somehow, our professors overlooked the lesson plans used in America's largest school district and our most likely employer.

Once I discovered there was no alternative to using the workshop model, I studied the format and immediately put it into practice. The lesson I discussed in an earlier chapter about writing strong thesis sentences was presented in the basic workshop model format. While a full lexicon of educational jargon would be needed to accurately describe the workshop model, to put it in parents' or taxpayers' terms, here's how it would be employed—and the thinking behind the execution—in a lesson on the use of figurative language in the early scenes of *Romeo and Juliet*.

Do Now (5–10 minutes). "We have studied similes and metaphors. List six examples each. (Here's a hint: 'A cloud of suspicion' is a metaphor. 'Hungry like the wolf' is a simile.)" While the kids settle down and write down various similes and metaphors, the teacher roams the room checking last night's homework and making sure the students are doing the Do Now. The class spends a few minutes reviewing what the students wrote down for the Do Now. This leads to…

Mini-Lesson (10–15 minutes). The teacher reviews types of figurative language and explains how it is used in Shakespeare. The teacher provides several good examples of figurative language in the beginning of the play. This is pretty much the teacher's big speaking part. There is no more lecturing. The teacher then becomes a facilitator of learning.

Group Work (15 minutes). Using the models the teacher provided in the Mini-Lesson, the students look for more figurative language in the first part of the play. Each group takes a piece of the beginning of the play, up through the meeting of Romeo and Juliet, and finds figurative language in that section.

Share (10 minutes). Each group reports to the class what they found in their section of the play and what makes it figurative language.

Summary (5 minutes). Teacher reviews what we learned.

Learning Log or Exit Slip (3 minutes). "Read this line from the play—'Love is a smoke made with the fume of sighs'—and answer yes or no whether it is figurative language. If yes, why? If no, why? Write the answer on a slip of paper and hand it in at the end of class." The teacher reviews these answers to see if the kids really did learn what they were supposed to learn.

Homework. "Take one of these worksheets on *Romeo and Juliet* as you leave and complete it tonight."

The Do Now gets the kids seated and warmed up to the topic. The Mini-Lesson gives the teacher a chance to talk and explain what we're learning, and model the work that the kids are supposed to do ("Find figurative language? Here are some examples..."). Then, the groups do the work, report on it so the whole class reviews it, and the teacher repeats what the class has learned. The exit slip shows if every kid has learned it, and the homework takes the lesson a little further.

Do this every day, 182 days a year, and you have a full curriculum and kids who probably have learned something.

What makes the workshop model so popular is that it becomes easy to "differentiate"—give each kid or group of kids work at the appropriate level. Some kids do work that's high on Bloom's Taxonomy, some lower. And a good teacher has so much input and data on each student that it's easy to figure out who is falling where and adjust their lessons and assignments accordingly.

The workshop model also uses cooperative learning—kids working in groups teaching each other. Don't forget, "Kids learn so much more from each other than they do from teachers" is a big mantra in education today. And it presents bite-size nuggets of learning in a short-attention-span format for a generation that has spent a lot of time snacking in front of a television set.

To Ms. P, the workshop model was not just a great idea; it was a fixed schedule for every period. If it's eighteen minutes into the period, the kids *will* be in Group Work. If the timing was off, Ms. P made clear, it was because the teacher had failed at some aspect of the lesson or classroom management. If Group Work didn't start until twenty-five minutes into the period, it meant that the students hadn't settled down and gotten to work immediately (poor classroom management), or the Do Now had taken too long (poor judgment of the scholars' cognitive level), or the Mini-Lesson had run on (teacher talks too much). In all, Ms. P's approach can be summed up in one word: choreography.

But for all the control, Ms. P could not—nor can any other administrator in the New York City system—tell the teacher precisely what to teach and how to teach it. There are topics to be covered, goals to be met, standards to be reached, but the actual lesson in the lesson plan is in the hands of the teacher. That is one of the few "Thank God!" work rules that the teachers' union has extracted from the city over the years. It allows teachers to use their professional judgment on some level and prevents them from being complete marionettes of the administration.

So, whether to study figurative language or teenage rebellion when reading *Romeo and Juliet* was up to the teacher, not Ms. P. But with this freedom came the responsibility of the teacher to get the needed results and cover the specific standards required by the city and the state. With that in mind, most teachers follow textbooks and model lessons, though constantly tweaking everything from required reading to activities, based on their experience with what works and doesn't with particular kids and classes.

Had it not been for the "academic freedom" clause in the city's contract with the teachers' union, there is little doubt that micromanaging principals such as Ms. P would have provided scripts to be followed, with each word and action prepared in advance. It sounds far-fetched, but Ms. P worked to limit the teachers' freedom under the guise of "best practices." After all, if data shows that saying these words and showing these PowerPoint slides and reading this excerpt at this pace and in this order improves student test scores, why should teachers be permitted to do it any other way?

The basic outline of the workshop model is used in school districts nationwide, at all income and achievement levels. There is, however, typically much more latitude in its execution elsewhere than in the New York City system. Though as data-backed "best practices" take hold around the country, I foresee a tightening of the reins on the teachers and the professional judgment of the individual educator becoming less important in lesson planning and delivery. I find it hard to believe that students will benefit more from the administration's best practices than from a teacher who is focused on their best interests.

BAD MOVES

In a 2012 nationwide study, 34 percent of teachers said they were anxious about keeping their jobs. In 2006, just 8 percent of teachers said they feared their jobs were insecure.

—28th Annual MetLife Survey of the American Teacher

THE THUMB DRIVE FULL of lesson plans and PowerPoints I'd received from the lead teacher was full of information for the ninth graders to copy off the Smart Board. And after trimming some of the longer, more complex material, I started the writing workshop with a unit on personal narrative. Yes, we were in compliance with New York State standards in ninth-grade English Language Arts—"Writing 3 a-e: Write narratives to develop real or imagined events."

In the first few weeks of the school year, we covered dramatic structure (narrative arc), the significant moment that gives a story its impact, how to come up with ideas, how to make a basic outline for a story, and, in addition to the kids copying stuff into their notebooks, there were handouts and read-alouds. We were off to a running start in terms of schoolwork, I thought. But between my animated manner and the students' boisterous response, I was seen by my superiors as weak on classroom management. I both wanted and needed to improve.

Everything I read about classroom management told me that routine and regularity are key, so I tried to keep things as consistent as possible. That was difficult, however, with school holidays and various assessment tests giving the kids breaks from class.

One day I received an email from Ms. P. It was marked with the red exclamation point of high priority. But already I had learned that everything—and that is not an exaggeration, *everything*—from Ms. P was marked with the red exclamation point of high priority.

Mr. Owens—
Would you like to attend the workshop in New Jersey? If so, we will pay for it.

Below the note was a promotional piece for a How to Teach Writing seminar that would be held in New Jersey in the weeks ahead. It was a daylong program in a hotel conference room with a buffet lunch and not an eighth or ninth grader in sight. The program promised a "unique, copyrighted approach to writing and thinking that offers much more than the standard writing process." I'm sure the program was excellent and the buffet lunch tasty, but the immediate benefit to my students wasn't clear.

Not only did I have decades of experience teaching people to write in an accessible style, but I also had the lesson plans and PowerPoints for a writing course from a man the lead teacher said was "the best teacher I ever knew." Most important of all, as I saw it, attending the program would have meant yet another day away from the routine and regularity that were supposed to be at the heart of good classroom management.

With that in mind, I responded:

Hello, Ms. P,

Thank you, I appreciate your thoughtfulness, but I will pass. For now, I would like to focus as much as possible on getting acquainted with the students and their skills.

John Owens

I should have known. That was a big mistake. Ms. P's reply:

You do not feel you need additional training? The assistant principal will be meeting with you to discuss this.

Before I could be hauled in by the assistant principal, I responded with a long, apologetic email about how I certainly needed more training, but that I didn't want to break the routine. My email was a humble act of contrition, obsequiousness, self-abasement, and deference.

Ms. P, in turn, sent me an email (copying the assistant principal) that sounded reasonable:

Thank you for emailing me back so that I have a clearer understanding of why you would rather not go. If there are any other opportunities later in the year I will notify you.

I breathed a sigh of relief, thinking the issue was settled, and redoubled my efforts to help the students and improve my own teaching skills.

But, in fact, this was a turning point. We went from having virtually no relationship to a negative one. Based on Ms. P's unwillingness to even look at me when we passed in the narrow halls, it was obvious that she now had me pegged as an ungrateful slacker who was unwilling to put himself out for the sake of professional growth. (Professional growth was one of her teacher non-negotiables.) Just weeks into the school year, I had gotten myself classified as a lazy sack of union-represented compost.

I got the impression that if it hadn't been for the fact that all teachers hired by the city are automatically members of the United Federation of Teachers, and that the union's contract specified that a new teacher couldn't be fired in the first year for anything short of violence or moral turpitude, I would have been canned on the spot.

Further turning Ms. P against me and accelerating my spiral into bad teacher hell was Kimber's mom. A bright boy who was quite a bit shorter than the other eighth graders, Kimber used his pixie good looks to full advantage, talking constantly, fast-balling whatever he could get his hands on, and roaming desk to desk like the maître d' of fifth period.

I asked him to sit down, moved his seat, even brandished my clipboard and pretended to write a report on his behavior. But each day—and many times each period—he would just smile impishly and do as he pleased. His own classwork got done, but the kids around him? They welcomed the distraction.

"Oh, it's that the girls are attracted to him, and they act up trying to get his attention. That's the problem. Other teachers have told me that," said his mother when I called to "conference."

I had hoped she would promise to speak with Kimber about his behavior in my class, but instead, she told me that I had trouble spotting the real problem, and that I was going to have to learn to cope with the fallout of her son's intoxicatingly magnetic good looks. A couple of weeks later, I discovered that Kimber's mom had pegged me for a racist, too.

"Please sign the original and keep the copy," the assistant principal said one afternoon, handing me a manila folder. Inside was a letter from Ms. P to me.

It concerned parent-teacher night, which took place two weeks into the term. In a classroom decorated with Big Brains, vocabulary words, and neatly arranged rows of books, I gave each of the couple-dozen adults who showed up a copy of the three-page syllabus and discussed how I would be pushing the students toward academic achievement and college-preparedness. But I knew that I wouldn't be any more than a Smart Board-flashing baby-sitter if I couldn't get the kids to sit down and do something resembling schoolwork. In other words, classroom management.

So, in my little talk to the parents, I also stressed how important it is for the students to behave, be quiet, and focus on their work to receive the best education possible, and how the parents could help their students do that. I told them how I had observed a class in a suburban school district where the kids just came in, sat down, and got to work, and how far the students were able to advance in their learning because of that.

"They don't waste any time on discipline. By the end of the year, those students are getting so much more instructional time," I told them. "Those kids aren't smarter. I think the kids at Latinate are smarter. But they are wasting a lot less time and getting more teaching time. Please, stress to your children how important it is to their education and their future success to behave in class." By sharing this anecdote, my hope was that it would inspire the parents to impress upon their kids the importance of good behavior and thus help me help their kids learn.

Opening the manila folder handed to me by the assistant principal, I saw the following letter:

Dear Mr. Owens:

We are giving you this letter to file for your failure to show cultural sensitivity to three parents during their visit to you on Curriculum Night on September 29, 2010. One parent, in particular, complained about your insensitive remarks comparing students from our school with those of Chappaqua with what she perceived as a racial subtext, i.e. that our students—predominantly African-American and Hispanic—do not do as well academically as the predominantly Caucasian students in the suburbs. The parent felt offended and disturbed by your remarks.... Your remarks, in whatever context they were given, were inappropriate and unprofessional. Consequently, we had to spend untold administrative hours on the phone with the parent to help resolve the issue and to assure the parent that this was an isolated incident that will not happen again. Please know that a recurrence of this type of behavior will be grounds for further disciplinary action including, but not limited to, an Unsatisfactory rating.

It didn't matter that I never mentioned race or Chappaqua, a place I've never been; this had sealed it. As far as Ms. P was concerned, I was officially, certifiably, and indisputably a bad teacher.

At first I was shocked. *What? This is crazy!* I thought, stunned by the blatant inaccuracies in this report.

"You can respond to this letter and I will put it in your file," the assistant principal said, bringing me to his desk where I was to sign the acknowledgment of Ms. P's missive. Still reeling from the bizarre accusation, I marked up a copy of the letter with my points of defense and handed it to the assistant principal. He read it, shrugged, slipped it into my file, and sent me on my way. Clearly, my rebuttal didn't have much of an impact. And anyway, once a letter was in the file, it didn't matter a whole lot whether the accompanying defense was good or bad. The letter still remained in the file.

Soon, shock gave way to anger.

"Ah, don't worry about it," my buddy, Ms. Lyons, told me when I regaled her with my tale at the end of the day. "The kids have called me racist, too."

"But you're black," I said.

"Yeah, I know." She smiled.

Then I began to feel horrible. My teaching career was off to a terrible, terrible start. Between not being able to tame the Natasha posse, declining the opportunity to further my professional development, and now being labeled a racist in a school where every student—as well as most of the staff—was black or Hispanic, it seemed I was well on the road to failure. Perhaps most disheartening was that I was being nailed for shortcomings in everything except what I thought I was here for—teaching these kids. Still, I wasn't about to give up. I was determined to salvage my career and redeem myself.

Before I became an officially bad teacher, it seemed that I had shown some promise. During the second week of school, an "informal" observation by the assistant principal had rated me as "Needs Improvement." In Ms. P's hierarchy of job-performance feedback, this was a notch above "Unsatisfactory" and a notch below "Satisfactory." But it was a start. The assistant principal came into the middle of one of my ninth-grade classes and noted that I provided "supportive feedback" and "continually reinforced appropriate behavior," and that the kids were not given any "free time."

Yes, I needed to make sure that the Do Now required a written response (not just copying); that even when I used a timer, I had to "make time more accountable"; and I had to become better at using a points system and having the kids see me mark down their points (or at least believe I did). But overall? I got the impression I didn't suck. My shortcomings didn't seem terminal, and I paid close attention to every point he raised. There were a lot. I wasn't delighted, but I was optimistic, confident that I could meet these criteria and earn a Satisfactory, at least with the ninth graders.

Suddenly, only a few more weeks into the term, that changed. The lead teacher and the assistant principal were in my classrooms so frequently that I should have put them on the attendance sheet. As they observed me at least once a week, what they found in my teaching was none too encouraging:

- "Start-of-class rowdiness."
- "Do Now takes too long."
- "Students off task."
- "Pacing" too slow ("free time = misbehaving!").
- Assignments lack "clarity" ("clear instructions: verbal & written").
- "All lessons should be data based. What data do you have to justify the teaching of the lesson aside from the fact that it is in your curriculum map?"
- "Since your students' notebooks are either disorganized or nonexistent, I was not able to find much archival evidence showing that you assess students' learning on a regular basis."
- "Yelling at the eighth graders."

Admittedly, progress with the wild eighth graders was slow, but the personal narrative unit in the ninth-grade writing workshop had been developing well. Or at least I thought so. We spent a couple of days spelling out exactly what were the definitions of the protagonist and antagonist of a story. ("We did this in sixth grade, too," complained Ron. "Yes, I know," I told him. "But some of the kids don't remember.")

We looked at "the good guy" (protagonist) and "the bad guy" (antagonist) in short stories, TV shows, and movies. We spent a lot of time discussing the 50 Cent film *Get Rich or Die Tryin'*, as well as Kevin James's ridiculously stupid movie, *Paul Blart: Mall Cop*, both of which everybody had seen and had thoughts on.

By the time I distributed worksheets on the topic, protagonists and antagonists seemed to be part of the family. The idea was for each kid to think about the protagonist and antagonist of the story he or she had outlined in the previous week and write down various details on the worksheets, one for the protagonist and another worksheet for the antagonist.

"List whatever you can think of about the antagonist and protagonist," I told them. "What is the protagonist's name? Age? Where does the protagonist live? Do the same for the antagonist." And so on. The kids asked lots of questions about what to put on the sheets, and I walked around the room as they worked.

In came Ms. P. She took a seat among the students at the back of the room. The report she filed tells the rest:

Mr. Owens—

When I entered the room, students had two worksheets in front of them, one that was labeled "antagonist" and one labeled "protagonist." I went around to six students, and every child gave me a different answer as to what they were supposed to be doing. One student said, "I am supposed to write a story and then complete the worksheets on the story." Another said, "I was given these questions for homework and now I have to fill out the worksheet." Another two students said, "I don't know what I am supposed to be doing." Another said, "My homework has nothing to do with the worksheets. I'm supposed to fill them out but I don't know why."

You did not establish clear expectations (purpose and product) for your students. Please remember students must be given clear and concise directions and must understand why they are working on the task. They need to have "the big picture." What is the purpose of this activity? How does this work connect to what they accomplished the prior day? How does this connect to the work they will be doing tomorrow or this week?

Improving the areas mentioned above will improve your lesson and student learning. If you would like to meet with me to discuss this observation further, please feel free to see my secretary for an appointment.

This observation was Unsatisfactory and will be placed in your official file.

Ms. P's report joined a five-pager from the assistant principal that found my work with the eighth grade Unsatisfactory. As the assistant principal pointed out, "There was no evidence of academic rigor (accountable talk and higher-order thinking skills)." Damn you, Bloom's Taxonomy!

The assistant principal had dispensed his Unsatisfactory rating based on the "Odyssey" lesson that opens this book. It was where I had the kids read the story in their textbook and watch a movie clip of Odysseus and his men encountering the Cyclops and then write down what happened. Getting the chronology, characters, and action right was a challenge for these eighth-grade students.

Nonetheless, my failure was that during this forty-six-minute period, I didn't push them beyond merely figuring out what was happening. Juxtaposing the behavior of Odysseus with the Cyclops, diagramming the motivations of the central players, or discriminating between truth and fiction in the dialogue would have been more suitable activities. But the students would not have understood how to do those without first understanding what was going on in the story. How to resolve such a dilemma?

As a result, Ms. P sent me a detailed memo that outlined a "Professional Development Plan" for the rest of the school year. I had to file lesson plans and blackboard configurations for each class, each day, each week, by the previous Friday at 5 p.m. I had to revise and update curriculum maps. I had to observe other teachers, write reports on what I saw, and meet with the assistant principal weekly so he could critique my teaching. After each meeting, I had to produce a reflective paragraph on how I would improve. I also was to have weekly coaching and meetings with the lead teacher as well as an outside consultant who would coach me.

A nightmare? No. Even the worst dreams don't require this much paperwork. But "nightmare" is the only way to explain having so many bosses. A public school teacher must answer to many constituents: school administration, the students, the parents, the taxpayers, the data, and the community at large. As a teacher at Latinate Institute, I was at the bottom of an organizational chart that had more arrows than Custer's Last Stand, and so many of the sharp ends were pointing at me.

I reported to Ms. P, our founding principal, of course; then the assistant principal; the lead teacher; my consultant-coach; the custodial staff (who wielded memos about my messy eighth graders); the teachers in the blue school on the second floor of the building (who regularly complained about the noise coming from the third floor as the eighth graders went about the stomping, desk-crashing, door-slamming business of middle school); as well as easily upset mothers, such as Nestor's litigious mom who had elicited a "Be careful!" warning from the assistant principal, and Kimber's mom, who while not much at disciplining her kid, considered herself quite adept at spotting racists.

Most importantly, I had virtually no leverage over the kids. I couldn't send miscreants out of the room, and it was a clear policy that teachers were responsible for handling all behavior problems within the class. And when it came to the eighth graders, I was having a hell of a time. I couldn't find any combination of sternness, humor, or calls home that made them put their phones down, stop talking, and refrain from throwing things and leaving the classroom at will, and even the helpful advice from my colleagues didn't work.

I was stumped. I tried interesting lessons (stories about war, poems about injustice, funny videos, more bloody videos, inspiring videos, and the daily eighty-word opinion pieces on outrageous topics that were taking off so well in the ninth-grade class). I even tried coloring. (We made flipbooks of our personal heroes.) But I still couldn't get the eighth graders as quiet and attentive as Ms. P demanded.

"Controlled chaos is not acceptable," the assistant principal told me one October afternoon when he was critiquing my performance. "You have to control the class with force of your personality."

Ah, yes! The force of my personality. I might not be a badass, but I could show them that there were consequences to their disruptions.

The next day, I told my rowdy eighth-period eighth graders that unless they quieted down, I would hold them after school. It didn't work. Tried again. And again. Finally, as the school day ended, I stood by the door.

"No one is leaving." I said. "You're all staying after school for ten minutes."

Kaboom! There was an eruption of anger, swearing, yelling, fist-pounding, and foot-stomping.

"You can't do that."

"I'm leaving! I wasn't talking."

"I have to go pick up my sister."

It seemed all the kids were out of their seats.

One usually quiet student, Raoul, stood in front of me visibly shaking with anger. I was certain he was going to attack me. "You can't do this!" he said, his teeth clenched.

I stood by the door to block anyone from grabbing the handle. The thick steel door in Room 321 was different from any other in the school. Rather than having a window in the center, it had a narrow pane of wire-reinforced glass on the side near the hinges. So, standing by the door handle, I couldn't see out the window into the hall.

"Open the door!" one of the girls yelled into my ear after looking out the narrow slit into the hall. "It's the assistant principal!"

I opened the door only to find Rico, a mischievous eighth grader, standing in the hall with a "gotcha" grin. A couple of my students headed for the opening. I quickly shut the door. A few seconds later, there was a strong push from the outside.

"It's Mr. Bookbinder!" the kids shouted. Mr. Bookbinder also taught these eighth graders and used this room as his base.

Facing the chaotic classroom, with my back still pressing against the door, I eased my pressure just a little and turned my head to the crack. "It's okay, Mr. Bookbinder. I have it under control."

Amid all of the yelling of the kids, I didn't hear any response. But the pressure let off the door. I stood firm.

Six minutes…seven minutes…eight…

"It's Ms. P! Open the door, it's Ms. P!" the window-peeping girl shouted in my ear. Certain that I would open the door only to see Rico again, I didn't move.

"You're staying for ten minutes! I don't care who's out there." And paraphrasing that old Jack Lord line from *Hawaii Five-O*, I added, "Nobody in. Nobody out."

"He's serious," said one boy.

"Sit down! So when the ten minutes are up, he'll have to let us go," growled Raoul.

"Yeah! Sit down."

"Sit down…"

The kids headed to their seats.

Suddenly, there was a huge push against the door. So hard that it couldn't be Rico. I gave way.

In burst Ms. P.

"*What is going on here?*" she shouted, her huge mouth agape, her eyes bugging, and her long, thin eyebrows arched so high that they resembled treacherous vertical ski slopes.

The kids erupted again with a full dramatic account of everything that had taken place in the past eight and a half minutes. I could tell that I had overstepped "the force of my personality." And with Ms. P's forced entry into the room, I looked pretty damn foolish. I definitely had lost more than control of the situation.

In a normal situation, I would have tried to explain what was going on. But one did not explain to this principal. I turned to Ms. P. "That's it. Good-bye."

I walked out of the classroom.

An administrator with a very professional manner and a slight Jamaican accent intercepted me on the way out of the school. She tried to talk.

"No. Thank you. That's it. I'm out of here. Good-bye."

Later in the year, this administrator left in a similar manner, handing her keys to the custodian on the way out. But on this day, I handed mine to her as we walked down the corridor.

"I can't do anything right, as far as the principal is concerned," I told her. "Thank you, but good-bye."

The next day, I felt terribly guilty about walking out on the kids, especially my ninth graders. I also felt stupid for having invested time and money in becoming a teacher, only to quit a few weeks into the school year, so when the assistant principal called and wanted to know if I was coming back, I was very contrite.

"I would like to come back if I am welcome." I returned to duty the next day.

"We thought you quit," some of my ninth graders said.

"Well, here I am."

That was good enough for them. We were all back at school.

There was a disciplinary hearing in Ms. P's office at which she presented written statements from other teachers and administrators that I was a muttering madman who "lost it" and shouted "Nobody in! Nobody out!" But as my representative from the United Federation of Teachers pointed out, "losing it" is not a clinical term. So Ms. P settled for putting a letter in my file chockfull of words such as "dangerous," "unsafe," "alarmed," "barricaded," and "insubordinate" and including this statement:

A recurrence of a similar situation may result in further disciplinary actions which may include, but are not limited to, an Unsatisfactory rating.

What I didn't know at the time was that I had taken precisely the wrong tack with those eighth graders.

"Oh, you can't hold them all for detention," Mr. Rodriguez, the gifted, badass special-education teacher, told me later. "Teachers have been punishing those kids as a group for years, and they hate it. It works with the other eighth-grade classes, but not them."

As it turned out, the most important thing I didn't know about my eighth-period eighth graders was that so many of them were special-education students. That is, the kid might have ADHD or dyslexia or any number of other learning or behavior issues. In fact, major problems with reading or math often lead to behavior problems—Nestor, who did nothing but pretend to punch me and taunt girls with his make-believe penis, was an extreme example. At least eight of the kids in that eighth-period class had special-needs classifications. That's a full one-quarter of the class. Several more students in the class should have had that classification, but either they had slipped through the cracks or perhaps their parents were afraid of the stigma attached to a proper diagnosis.

For a kid with special needs, the personalized attention of a special-education teacher can help overcome years of problems, confusion, impatience, and being overlooked by the education system. In fact, in New York City, a class with classified students must have a special-ed teacher present. You wouldn't know that based on my experience at Latinate. Although nearly half the kids in one of my eighth-grade classes had serious learning or behavior problems, the school year was several months old before I even was informed about who the special-ed students were, and I had yet to glimpse a special-ed teacher in my eighth-grade class.

At Latinate, the special-ed team was stretched so thin because Ms. P had two of the four teachers also running French classes. The school was, after all, a college-preparatory institute, and "French" sounds a whole lot better on a curriculum than "legally mandated special-education."

Only now and then was my eighth-period, eighth-grade class visited by a special-ed teacher. Ms. Perker was a fresh Ivy League graduate with a caffeine-rich personality. A history major, she had spent a summer learning to be a special-ed teacher. Hardworking and sincere, Ms. Perker was, like the rest of us newbies, totally in over her head.

A special-ed teacher is not supposed to yell. Calm, firm, clear instructions and a no-nonsense attitude are essential. But Ms. Perker yelled. A special-ed teacher is not supposed to get mad when a student like Alec—the sixteen-year-old ninth grader who recently immigrated from the Dominican Republic without any (truly, any) English language skills—comes up behind you in class and makes his creepy, Spanish-inflected smooching sound. But Ms. Perker got mad.

There's also much to be said for a special-ed teacher who can move around the classroom with poise. But Ms. Perker traveled the room like the referee in a fast-moving basketball game. At this stage of her career, Ms. Perker had few of the required skills, but with so much demand for certified special-ed teachers, Ms. Perker was not an immediate target for Ms. P and her ubiquitous "Unsatisfactory" rating.

Ms. Perker was assigned to help me out in eighth period. The first time she arrived, she roamed the classroom helping to keep the kids on track. *Shhh*ing, looking stern, and tapping on the desk, she had my total support, since she improved not only the teacher-student ratio, but also the teacher-student odds. Unfortunately, that didn't last long.

"Oh, I can't make it today," Ms. Perker told me on what was to be Day Two of her legally mandated presence. "I have to cover for someone."

So it went most of the time—Ms. Perker being assigned to almost anything during eighth period except my class. I started keeping track of how many times she was there, but gave up when there weren't many to track.

When special ed comes on an "as available" basis, everyone suffers. The kids who need the extra help and attention don't get it, and if anything from ADHD to the frustration of not being able to do the work causes them to act out, the learning of the whole class is disrupted.

JUDGMENT DAZE

Today, half the states require at least some objective measure of student achievement as part of teacher evaluations, and twelve make it the most significant factor.

—*USA Today*, March 21, 2012

ONE OF THE KEY issues in school reform is how to evaluate teachers' effectiveness—demonstrating clearly, and ideally with data, who is a good teacher and who is a bad teacher. Some of those involved in school reform even suggest using this information to help the bad teachers improve. Others prefer the option of just firing them and bringing in fresh blood. The fundamental question, however, still remains: how do you evaluate teachers fairly and accurately?

One increasingly popular approach is called "value-added modeling" (VAM).* Developed in the 1980s by statistician William

---

*The RAND Corporation has studied this statistical technique's use in education for more than a decade. For a reasonably impartial explanation of it—as well as a look at how it can be abused—see the article "The Promise and Peril of Using Value-Added Modeling to Measure Teacher Effectiveness" at rand.org/pubs /research_briefs/RB9050/index1.htmla window.

Sanders, VAM, as a 2003 report by the RAND Corporation defined it, is "a collection of complex statistical techniques that use multiple years of students' test-score data to estimate the effects of individual schools or teachers."

Since 1993, Tennessee has used a value-added assessment system developed by Sanders. According to the state, this mathematical model "reveals academic growth over time for students and groups of students, such as those in a grade level or in a school." This data, based on students' scores on standardized state tests, "is a tool that gives feedback to school leaders and teachers on student progress and assesses the influence of schooling on that progress…[and] provides valuable information for teams of teachers to inform instructional decisions."

Despite the state's assurances of accuracy and fairness, along with nearly two decades of use, Tennessee's VAM system remains controversial with educators and mathematicians who question its worth as a gauge of teacher efficacy. But in 2012, for the first time, this mathematical model was used to rate the state's teachers based on whether their students made significant gains on standardized tests.

While Tennessee also uses other criteria—including classroom observations—to judge a teacher's overall job performance, VAM has gained nationwide attention as a way to attach data to the teacher's productivity. After all, there's a lot of appeal in data that supporters believe can, at a glance, reveal how much "value" a teacher adds to—or subtracts from—each student's performance.

As a result, VAM systems are being embraced across the nation, with Florida, Texas, California, Pennsylvania, Ohio, and Washington, D.C., among those crunching the numbers. America's largest school system, New York City, does, too. President Barack Obama's Race to the Top, which provides awards to states that advance school reform, also has a value-added component.

Though all use mathematical modeling, not all VAM systems are the same. They vary in the data they analyze (most use annual state exams) as well as how far they push the mathematical models. Some systems merely rate student progress. Others, such as the model tested in New York City, predict future performance. That is, the model looks at students' past years' performance and then predicts their future scores.

If, ultimately, the kids do better than predicted, their teacher is a good teacher. If the students perform worse than the model predicted, their teacher is a bad teacher. And gradations of good and bad can be assigned report-card-style grades or ratings of "high," "above average," "below average," and "low."

The problems with this are not just philosophical—the responsibility for each child's learning now shifted from the student to the teacher—but also mathematical. Unreliable data and statistical flukes are numerous. When New York City released data on 18,000 teachers in early 2012, the grades were accompanied by a caveat from the DOE that the margin of error in a teacher's math score could be 35 percentage points, and 53 points on the English exam. In other words, the ratings were meaningless because the DOE hadn't yet figured out how to gather a sufficient quantity of statistically reliable numbers to crunch.*

The real issue is that these numbers can be skewed by factors

---

*As Charles Seife points out in his delightful explanation of statistics, *Proofiness: How You're Being Fooled by the Numbers* (Penguin, 2010), "The margin of error can be considered as pretty much nothing more than how big the sample is." And "the larger the sample, the less error there is due to random weirdness." Scientific research typically aims for a sample size large enough to keep the margin of error in the three-percent range. Polls? Five percent is common. The 35 and 53 percent margins of error in the teacher grades reflect sample sizes so tiny that the numbers hardly are statistics at all.

ranging from a small sample size (just a few kids in the class for whom there's data) to kids who happen to advance rapidly in one or two years but then level off. In the latter case, it's virtually impossible for the students to keep moving ahead in their learning at that rate, so their strong early performance ends up penalizing their teacher in later years. In essence, the data says that this teacher isn't as good as he or she used to be, because the students aren't advancing as quickly. Then, of course, there's the possibility of anyone on up to top education officials tampering with the test scores, of which there have been a number of highly publicized cases.

Clearly, as with value-added grades in many parts of the country, New York's teacher ratings are too new and too unreliable to be taken seriously. As the *New York Times* reported Feb. 24, 2012:

> The release of the individual rankings [for New York City teachers] has been even controversial among the scientists who designed them. Douglas N. Harris, an economist at the University of Wisconsin, where the city's rankings were developed, said the reports could be useful if combined with other information about teacher performance. But because value-added research is so new, he said, "we know very little about it." Releasing the data to the public at this point, Dr. Harris added, "strikes me as at best unwise, at worst absurd."

But try downplaying the merit of these rankings to a parent whose child's teacher gets anything but the highest grade. Where disclosed, teacher ratings are generally available on websites, making them nearly as obvious and impactful as the Board of Health grades posted outside restaurants.

While teachers and parents have long been allies in the

fight for better schools, for more resources for their children and students, and for support for better education and learning opportunities, value-added grades could disrupt that relationship, setting parents against teachers (*"What is my child doing with a C-rated teacher?"*). In fact, it could be argued that education is so important that any teacher who falls below the highest level is a bad teacher. And in that case, there certainly will be ample data proving that America's schools are "infested" with bad teachers. That's how Michelle Rhee, previously mentioned, read the data as chancellor of the Washington, D.C., public schools in her 2010 firing of 241 teachers, most of whom had received the lowest rating on an evaluation system that made them responsible for their students' standardized test scores. While Tennessee promotes these ratings as a way to provide "valuable information for teams of teachers to inform instructional decisions," it's obvious how they can be abusive weapons in the hands of tyrannical reformers such as Rhee and Ms. P.

The result could be a fundamental shift in both American culture and politics. If school reformers can persuade parents that their children deserve only A-rated teachers and that only reform can ensure that, America's teachers will have lost their loudest and most numerous supporters—the grassroots moms and dads of schoolchildren. The vast majority of teachers are not only capable but excellent educators, but that shift of allegiances would leave them virtually friendless and powerless. I find it hard to believe that administrators—especially those who stand to earn a bonus as well as those working for any of the increasing number of public schools operated by for-profit corporations—would be better, more honest advocates for children.

The good news, however, is that the VAM proponents don't have the facts on their side. Mathematician John Ewing published a critique of value-added modeling in the May 2011 issue of *Notices of the American Mathematical Society*, calling VAM "an exceedingly blunt tool" for evaluating teachers. He asked:

> Why must we use value-added even with its imperfections?... [T]he only apparent reason for its superiority is that value-added is based on data. Here is mathematical intimidation in its purest form—in this case, in the hands of economists, sociologists, and education policy experts.

Ewing, who is president of Math for America, a private, nonprofit organization with a mission to improve math education in secondary public schools, ended his analysis with a call to action:

> Unlike many policy makers, mathematicians are not bamboozled by the theory behind VAM, and they need to speak out forcefully. Mathematical models have limitations. They do not by themselves convey authority for their conclusions. They are tools, not magic. And using the mathematics to intimidate—to preempt debate about the goals of education and measures of success—is harmful not only to education but to mathematics itself.

Though value-added modeling is rapidly gaining ground nationwide, so far it is the determining factor in only a tiny number of teacher evaluations. Across America, as in New York City during my time at Latinate, observation reports from the principal and assistant principal are, for the time being, the most important factor in judging teacher performance.

With that in mind, the Bill & Melinda Gates Foundation has

developed a teacher-evaluation system that is driven by observation, albeit with a data-intensive twist. After videotaping 3,000 teachers in action at schools around the country, Gates Foundation researchers say they have identified teacher practices that are "associated with student achievement." Recording the teachers' use of these practices, along with principal, teacher, and student evaluations of each teacher's work, as well as test scores, will give a clearer picture of a teacher's worth and effectiveness, says Gates. And, the billionaire reformer and philanthropist insists, this system will give teachers information they need to improve their teaching, not just look for another line of work.

So far, the Gates approach is being tested in pilot programs in four school districts, with the foundation dispensing hundreds of millions of dollars to these districts over nearly a decade. Gates is right when he says that there's no merit in shaming teachers with ratings based only on student test-score data (as New York City did). But the system he is exploring might be too complicated and expensive to implement for many schools, since it calls for highly trained observers and evaluations that go far beyond just gut feeling and a checklist.

The Gates approach also is still too embryonic to know if it can be manipulated by administrators. After all, in theory, Ms. P's teacher observations also were objective and designed to help teachers improve. But in practice, they were highly subjective and capable of turning in any result that Ms. P wanted. Furthermore, Gates' idea of identifying teacher practices that boost student achievement could be distorted by administrators such as Ms. P who ignore or misinterpret the nuances of instruction and teacher-student interaction, instead turning Gates' "best practices" into a set of strict rules that must be followed or else.

The observation system I encountered at Latinate was

supposed to help me become a better teacher. And the earliest reports and meetings with both the assistant principal and lead teacher, although very critical, were helpful. But once the principal took a dislike to me, the tenor of the observation reports became decidedly negative and discouraging. It became clear to me that Ms. P & Co. weren't so much interested in making me a good teacher as proving I was a bad teacher. After a while, everything about the help I received had a tone of evidence, a paper trail that would stand as proof of my incompetence.

All paperwork a teacher receives in the New York City system requires a signature acknowledging receipt. Early on, the signature line was accompanied by the standard, benign sentence, "I acknowledge receipt of this communication and understand that a copy will be placed in my file."

But once Ms. P decided I had crossed the line into the realm of being a bad teacher, the closing at the signature line became this all-caps message:

FAILURE TO RETURN SIGNED COPIES ON THE SAME DAY WILL MEAN THAT YOU HAD REFUSED TO SIGN AND IT WILL BE INDICATED ON THE COPY AS SUCH.

Ms. P's "Formal Observation Expectations Checklist" was a three-page, single-spaced form with sixty-six criteria that were simultaneously so detailed and convoluted ("Classroom practices reflect teacher awareness and utilization of available data, e.g., biographical/attendance/disciplinary data, state and city assessment data, ARIS data, in-house baseline-interim-end line data, etc.") and so subjective ("Executes lessons well with excellent pacing and focus; makes instruction interesting and compelling"; "Students give eye contact to the teacher while s/he is teaching") that it seemed that only through the grace of Ms. P could anyone get sufficient check marks to be deemed a satisfactory pedagogue.

I quickly found that with so many criteria and so much subjective wiggle room on which to judge a teacher's performance, it wasn't tough for Ms. P to prove anything she wanted to prove.

By mid-October, I was spending a good deal of my nonteaching time in meetings receiving critiques of my performance from the assistant principal and the lead teacher. Never together: each of them worked me over separately. And each time, the assistant principal instructed me to provide him with a reflection on what we had discussed. By "reflection," he meant a memo saying, "Yes, you are right—there were shortcomings in my lesson as you pointed out, and here's how I intend to remedy this."

But realizing that these memos would be put into my official file, I was hesitant to admit anything that could and—knowing Ms. P—*would* be used against me. So my reflections were positive and upbeat, stressing the strengths of my lessons, the engagement of the students who were paying attention, and the ways in which I could make it even better next time.

When he saw these, the assistant principal shook his head in what appeared to be disappointment and pity at my inability to follow instructions. "You are just starting as a teacher," he said in tone of quiet counsel. "You can't afford to get a U. If you do, you will be out of the System. You will never be able to teach in New York City again."

"I know," I said, eager to avoid that fate. "I don't want to get a U."

"She has given me a U," he said of Ms. P. "But I am at the end of my career, and it doesn't make that much difference. For you, however…"

"What? Ms. P gave *you* a U?" I said incredulously, referring to his ten-hour days, six-day work weeks, and status as her top henchman.

"Yes," he sighed. "She *is* demanding. That's why you must cooperate."

This is crazy, I thought. The assistant principal often dropped comments about his financial plight ("I sold my car; I couldn't afford it"; "I'd like to get a computer like that, but I don't have $800"). And to keep the paychecks coming, he took whatever abuse the principal dished out. Including the ultimate slap a New York City educator can receive: Unsatisfactory ratings. That was sad enough. But that he was trying to recruit me, telling me that the only way I could save my career was to put myself at the mercy of the merciless Ms. P...

"Cooperate, huh?" I said, stunned but noncommittal.

That performance reviews could be so subjective and political didn't surprise me. That's the way the world—both in schools and elsewhere—often operates. It certainly has been that way in every organization I've ever encountered. But amid America's mania to root out bad teachers, it's now especially easy for administrators to settle personal and political scores under the cover of teacher accountability.

At Latinate, the word "cooperate" had little to do with classroom performance and student learning. It meant putting your career totally in Ms. P's hands, as well as giving her all of your spare time. In other words, *volunteer.*

In truth, I really didn't have much life left to volunteer. The soft life of a teacher was taking every waking hour and then some. I really was pouring my heart and soul into the lesson plans, the PowerPoints, and the calls and emails to the parents. I really was putting up bulletin boards showing exemplary student work—and even included the appropriate evaluation rubrics, as Ms. P's bulletin board standards required. And I really was reading the students' papers with care and concern not just for grammar, spelling, and structure, but also for content, especially cries for help, which I saw with sad and alarming frequency.

The kids loved to write about themselves—their likes, their dislikes, their experiences, their feelings about their aunt's dog ("So cute!"), their reaction to their sister's runny nose ("Gross!"). I made it a point to assign them pieces about themselves, but it didn't matter; they had a way of turning every assignment into writing about themselves. And as long as they were writing, it was fine by me.

My students' cleverness at doing the assignment while denying they were doing it—and yet still demanding credit for doing it—was quite impressive. For instance, one day, the eighth graders' homework was to write eighty words about their most memorable moment and describe it using their five senses. Enid, who was bright, energetic, and an ingenious though clumsy cheater on the weekly vocabulary tests, provided this doing, not doing, yet doing submission:

> I don't know any memorable moment. Right now I have writer's block, so I don't remember anything to write about. And I'm tired and sleepy. Everyone in the house is sleeping and it is quiet, so I can hear the refrigerator running. Oh, wait! I have something: Since I was bored today, I decided to bite off my fingernails. They smell like skin. They look short, sharp, and crooked. They taste like the medicine I just put on my brother.

Ciphering along the margin notified me that this piece was exactly eighty words. I chuckled when I saw the math and had to admire her literal as well as literary achievement. It added up to a writer's imagination combined with an attorney's argumentativeness. She got a "check plus plus"—my highest homework rating—in acknowledgment of her effort without seeming to "try." It was a start, and I hoped it would encourage even better work from her.

Much of the writing, however, was darker and sadder. Rikkie, the bright, defiant ninth grader, did a long piece about how prison isn't so bad. He knew this because his father had told him in phone calls from the penitentiary in upstate New York. "It's like being in the army," he said in the essay. "You wear uniforms, there are a lot of rules, and you can't leave." (Not unlike Latinate, a cynic might say.) "The food is good," Rikkie wrote. "All you want."

One ninth-grade girl wrote about the day she saw her father get arrested in the neighborhood check-cashing store. Another wrote about the day her cousin was shot and killed on a playground in upper Manhattan, and how she wore his photograph on a cord around her neck. A boy in the same class wrote about how his girlfriend was pregnant and he was soon going to be a father.

When our work on protagonists and antagonists led to writing fiction, Keena, a tall, heavyset, ninth-grade girl who called me "Mr. Owens, My Favorite Teacher," handed in a story about a girl who was attacked and raped by her father while she slept. The details in the story (the smell of his breath, the feel of his hands, her surprised, eyes-kept-shut reaction) were as chilling as the topic.

Keena was a bright kid, but this was so real it almost couldn't have been created so well unless she really had experienced this or something much like it. Somehow it seemed more than a product of a remarkably vivid imagination. Suspecting this wasn't a piece of fiction, I took it to the lead teacher and asked her how to proceed with the school social worker.

"Oh, don't worry about it. It's not real. Our kids love to write about that sort of thing."

"Are you sure?" I asked, thinking back to my time as a police reporter for a newspaper in upstate New York where I discovered that the most heinous things can and do happen with surprising frequency.

"Yes," she insisted, giving me a Ms. P-style flutter of the hand to shoo me away.

So I let it drop, sensing I was becoming almost as much of a nuisance as the garrulous Mr. Bookbinder and committing the Latinate felony of "wasting the administration's time."

I was trying, and I was working—I thought—really, really hard. And it seemed that many of the kids were enjoying my class and making progress. But Ms. P wanted more. She wanted activities, dances, trips…anything to add dimension to the pageant she was creating at Latinate. The New York City Department of Education proudly states on its teacher-recruiting website that after-school and weekend work earns teachers $41.98 per hour. Ms. P, however, always pleaded a lack of budget and asked for "volunteers."

"I figure I will work here at the school until 9 o'clock every night for three years," a second-year special-ed teacher told me, "I'll make Ms. P happy and then I will get tenure."

Of course, unless she then transferred to another school, even tenure wouldn't protect that teacher from the demands of the U-wielding Ms. P. She only had to look at the misery of the long-tenured Mr. Bookbinder and even-longer-tenured Ms. Patel.

Two other beginning teachers were better at volunteering than I was. Ms. Nenza, the fresh-from-graduate-school English teacher, and Mr. Steinman, a young, eager social studies teacher, were appointed eighth- and twelfth-grade class advisors. Since they were moving up from middle school, the eighth graders, like the twelfth graders, were considered "seniors." That meant a yearbook, a prom, and a class trip. Ms. Nenza and Mr. Steinman quickly assumed duties as editors, publishers, party planners, travel agents, and fund-raisers for their respective classes. An overnight trip to a Connecticut theme park for fifty-plus eighth graders and a two-night excursion to Washington, D.C., for nearly as many twelfth graders were just the start. An evening aboard a dinner-cruise yacht sailing around Manhattan provided the class prom and was, said Ms. P, a Latinate "ritual."

Between caps and gowns, trips, parties, and yearbooks, each eighth- and twelfth-grade senior was incurring potentially hundreds of dollars in graduation expenses. Here's how it was presented to the eighth-grade "seniors" in a class-wide handout:

- Package 1: Senior Dues and Yearbook, $90
    Student will *only* attend the graduation ceremony
    5 payments of $18 each
- Package 2: Senior Dues, Yearbook, and Senior Prom, $200
    Student will *not* attend the Senior Trip
    5 payments of $40 each
- Package 3: Senior Dues, Yearbook, and Senior Trip, $270
    Student will *not* attend the Senior Prom
    5 payments of $54 each
- Package 4: Senior Dues, Yearbook, Senior Trip, and Senior Prom, $380
    Student will participate in *all* activities
    5 payments of $76 each

I was stunned to see this. In a school where almost every student receives a free or low-cost lunch due to family finances, it struck me as reckless to ask these kids and their families to foot the bill. Latinate sits in a slice of New York City that holds the dubious distinction of being the poorest Congressional district in the United States. The 2010 U.S. Census reported a median household income of $23,773 in this part of the Bronx— $4,424 below the second-poorest, southeastern Kentucky's Fifth Congressional District.

The lack of money in the neighborhood is signaled most clearly by the lack of real banks. I did not see even one in the area around Latinate. These days, the huge, granite bank buildings that dominated busy corners from the 1920s through the 1950s—when the Bronx was viewed as a borough of upward strivers—are either makeshift churches or have faded signs offering the property for sale or lease.

The role of the bank has been taken by check-cashing stores or, even more commonly, bodegas. Whether the sign over the awning says "Bodega," "Grocery," "Deli," "Food Market," "Superette," "Quickie," or "Mart," they all are brightly lit explosions of colorful commercialism plastered with a haphazard array of signs announcing Lotto, ATM, Newport cigarettes, Cold Beer, We Accept WIC (a federal program that provides food checks for pregnant women and small children), as well as Grill Open, and photos of various sandwiches that can be quickly prepared, wrapped in waxed paper, and stuffed into a brown paper bag.

More than a corner store in the South Bronx, the bodega is an essential part of life—and financial life—especially for those on the move outside normal business hours. Where do you get coffee at 7 a.m.? Disposable diapers at 11 p.m.? A money order at midnight? Or cash from an ATM just about any time? The bodega.

Cash the kids weren't spending at bodegas on sandwiches, Skittles, Jolly Ranchers, and AriZona Iced Tea was targeted by the seniors' fund-raising events. There was a steady parade of dances, dress-down days (pay a few dollars to the senior class and you don't have to wear the school uniform for a day), and candy-bar sales throughout the school (two dollars to ingest a handful of high-octane sugar just minutes before Mr. Owens's eighth-grade English class). But it still left each eighth and twelfth grader having to pay hundreds.

Ms. P's solution? Not unlike any merchant in a low-income neighborhood, she arranged an installment payment plan for the students, as the handout to the eighth-grade seniors showed. Five easy payments of $76 and you have prepaid your graduation. With a trip, yearbook, and cap and gown in the balance, the pay-up rate was high.

The hours Ms. Nenza and Mr. Steinman put into these efforts were astounding. While they were chaperoning fund-raising dances, I was at home creating PowerPoints for upcoming classes. While they were arming the students with candy bars that the kids hustled around the school, I was trying to get all of my classes up to date on the electronic grading system. They, too, faced all of these challenges and demands of pedagogy and paperwork. And there's no doubt that they met their obligations. So I can only figure that they didn't sleep. They told me as much, and most days, I noticed Mr. Steinman arriving at school and rushing down the hall with a frazzled and disheveled look, as though he'd been boosted out of bed by someone shouting "Fire!"

If I had found any time or energy to volunteer, I would have preferred using it to teach Albert, my smiling, courteous eighth grader, to read. Or helping the polyglot Ahmad get more out of the time he spent with honor student Mark. Of course, I also could say that if I had had the time and energy I would have learned to play the piano and speak Italian. After a full day at Latinate and an evening grading, preparing, data-compiling, data-crunching, and reflecting, I had neither the hours nor the oomph. I felt like I was, unquestionably, a bad teacher.

Both Ms. Nenza and Mr. Steinman were hard workers and good teachers. They cared, they tried, and they were able to squeeze more hours from a day than I could. But from what I saw, they were no better in the classroom than I was. No better at all. We watched each other work quite a bit, and we shared many of the same students. All three of us—like any new teachers— were riding a wild bull every time we stepped into a classroom. But it didn't take deep analysis to see that the most important criterion on Ms. P's sixty-six-point formal observation expectations checklist had little to do with in-class performance. It was the unwritten Number 67—"Volunteering to Promote the Pageant of Today's Successful School." And my performance in that regard was wanting.

The result was that in mid-January, both Ms. Nenza and Mr. Steinman received critical though nonetheless Satisfactory reviews of their teaching. They had a "future" (or at least one more year) in the System. With my Unsatisfactory ratings, I was an example and a warning to other teachers. However, the one saving grace for the stability of my kids was that I couldn't be fired right away.

As I mentioned earlier, in New York City, unless a newcomer is caught in heinous activity of a violent or sexual nature (not merely Unsatisfactory classroom performance and failure to cooperate), the teacher is permitted to work through the school year. That doesn't mean the bad teacher's life can't be made miserable along the way. By December, I was experiencing the punishment for my lack of extra volunteering in the form of even more critiques of my teaching and a virtually nonstop stream of advice and coaching.

Even the tenured teachers were expected to devote their spare time to Ms. P's pet projects. One math teacher was charged with updating the school website that had been set up in addition to the standard site provided by the Department of Education. Another teacher oversaw the various data-recording websites that all teachers had to use, as well as put together PowerPoint presentations Ms. P could show at staff and PTA meetings, while yet another organized and distributed numerous state and city standard exams.

Ms. Lyons was able to escape the school each afternoon and return to her home far north of the city without incurring Ms. P's wrath. Yes, Ms. Lyons had strong classroom management and data-gathering skills, but more importantly, she also had an education administrator's license that allowed her to handle the dense financial paperwork of the DOE.

Each day, she spent her professional period (as well as some additional time) as the purchasing manager for Latinate. As a competent professional slicing through the bureaucracy that paid for everything from textbooks to toilet paper, Ms. Lyons was very, very valuable to the Ms. P regime. In simplest terms, she was performing the most vital service of all—saving the administration's time.

From December on, the assistant principal was regularly sitting in my classes with a laptop computer assessing every move I made, from making sure that no kids were out of uniform ("Where's your tie? I need you to wear your tie or you'll get detention") to making sure that each student wrote down each day's homework assignment and that I stamped each student's book when it was written down. We then reviewed his observations in a weekly meeting. When the lead teacher observed my classes, she used a stopwatch to measure how long I spent on each part of the lesson. ("Seven minutes on the Do Now is way too long.")

But I was improving. I was especially good with the ninth graders. Even the lead teacher had to admit it. She not only told me so, but also wrote up a compliment that said, "Your Do Now and homework are highly engaging to the students and they clearly are engaged with the whole-class text. You're connecting their life to their text; and expecting them to be able to explain and defend themselves."

Although these positive words were followed on the same sheet of paper by a critique of my performance with the eighth graders ("sends the message to the rest of the class that you *can't* control the room/students"), I was delighted with the praise. I noted, however, that this paperwork didn't go into my official file, since it wasn't presented to me for the acknowledging signature, which would have been required.

Ironically, despite constant moaning about a lack of budget, Ms. P hired a retired high school principal to coach me and several tenured teachers who were falling short of her expectations.

While the tenured teachers took the coach's presence as yet another slap from Ms. P, as a tyro I found his advice good and his manner reassuring. He worked with me on my out-of-control eighth-period eighth graders—the class that only occasionally had the special-ed teacher the law required. He helped me a great deal with classroom management, and I got the sense that he really wanted me to be a good teacher.

I welcomed his guidance. I imagined that this was what it would be like to work in a school where new teachers were valued and mentored. The coach's written reports were full of positive encouragement—even when addressing areas for improvement. I started to get excited at the prospect of real improvement in my teaching and classroom management—improvement that might impress even the formidable Ms. P.

But there was one problem: nobody coordinated with the coach or each other what they told me to do and not to do.

"Let the kids read out loud," said the coach.

"Never let the kids read out loud," said the lead teacher. "Our kids don't read well enough."

"Let the kids chat while you go around and check homework," said the coach.

"It must be totally silent while you go around and check homework," said the lead teacher.

"Your energy and enthusiasm are great," said the coach. "You have a lively, enthusiastic, even theatrical, manner and presentation. This helped at times to engage and focus your students as you read part of the story to them."

"Don't be so energized and enthusiastic. It riles up the kids," said the lead teacher.

I was baffled. Whose advice was I supposed to follow? Mind you, to a layperson, these distinctions may seem small, but at Latinate they were the difference between a certifiably good teacher and, well, me. And I was desperate to be a good teacher. When professors from Empire State College stopped by Latinate to observe my classes for my master's of teaching program, they were positive and encouraging.

Yes, they saw beginner mistakes and the usual first-year teacher problems with classroom management. For instance, I had a tough time getting the kids to immediately get to work upon entering the room—even with the official timer. I also had trouble redirecting kids who were off-topic without drawing attention to them. I was supposed to use body language, gestures, and other nonverbal cues to make the kids behave. I was a rookie. But was I "bad"? No. Like the coach, my college instructors (one of whom was a retired teacher) had helpful advice and practical ideas that I was eager to implement.

For instance, like the coach, they told me to ignore minor disruptions and "side chatter."

"It usually self-extinguishes and stops naturally on its own," the coach said. "Try not to publicly admonish, correct students who are disruptive, or place their names on the board for detention. This calls attention to their negative behavior, embarrasses them, and leads to needless commentary and power struggles."

"But what about the silent cathedral of learning?" I asked.

He made a "What are you talking about?" face, but then, as though he suddenly remembered who was paying him, he paused. "Well, try to circulate around the room and use proximity to the disruptive students," he said. "Maybe indicate to them that you will speak with them later."

I really wanted to be—and go on as—a teacher. But it wasn't to be. My teaching wasn't the problem. Or, more accurately, the *real* problem. Instead, I had the bad judgment, bad form, and bad luck to have gotten off to a very bad start with the principal.

Nonetheless, my experience shows how a seemingly professional and long-used teacher-evaluation tool—classroom observation—can be very subjective, as well as misused and manipulated by powerful, tyrannical administrators. Combining observations with data—whether in the form of value-added modeling or another mathematical approach—is probably no better. The flaws of mathematical models are just part of the problem. The data itself is often suspect, or it isn't necessarily an accurate measure of a teacher's effectiveness.

Another system—no doubt a brand-new system—must be developed to accurately evaluate teachers. While data will no doubt play a role, perhaps professional observers—impartial experts trained to evaluate teachers' performance—are part of the answer. But first and foremost, America must not go into this believing that all teachers are bad until proven otherwise.

Voices of Teachers around the Country

Mr. "X," Second Grade Teacher, Southwest Florida

In my district here in southwestern Florida, 50 percent of my final evaluation for the year will be based upon the test scores of children in grades four and five. I taught second grade this year. This is my first year at this school. So, in effect, half of my effectiveness as a teacher is to be determined by test scores from students I've *never* taught and most of whom I've *never* even met.

How anyone could keep a straight face and maintain any moral integrity while telling me that this is a fair system is beyond my understanding, yet this is the program that my betters in the district office produced, the State of Florida approved, and the U.S. Department of Education accepted as meeting the requirements of its Race to the Top program.

How could I have added value or subtracted value for students I've never even spoken to or been with in a classroom? Osmosis?

I've been teaching for fifteen years, always in high-needs schools. I hold two master's degrees and was named Social Studies Teacher of the Year for my district last year.

I fully expect my final rating to be "Needs Improvement" or "Ineffective" when the test scores are added in to my "value," since the state has raised the bar so high for passing and made the test far more difficult this year. My principal actually rated me "Highly Effective" based upon her numerous formal and informal observations and review of my teaching portfolio, but that only counts for half, so...

Now, after two years of low ratings in Florida, you lose your professional teaching certificate and can be fired at will. Looks like it's time to start looking for employment outside the school system. That makes me very sad and sick at heart, but I don't see anything changing for the better any time soon.

Mr. "X" first posted his story on DianeRavitch.net on June 2, 2012.

12

CHEATERS' PARADISE

Never before have so many [teachers and administrators] had so much reason to cheat. Students' scores are now used to determine whether teachers and principals are good or bad, whether teachers should get a bonus or be fired, whether a school is a success or failure.

—Michael Winerip, The *New York Times*, July 31, 2011

THE WEEKLY VOCABULARY TESTS I administered to my eighth- and ninth-grade English classes provided an example of the adolescent intellect at work. Not more than a handful of kids in each class bothered studying the ten to fifteen words they had been given Monday and we then reviewed on Tuesday, Wednesday, and Thursday, and which were also posted on the walls on colorful sheets of paper written in vibrant Sharpie. Instead, they put remarkable amounts of energy and cranial muscle into cheating on the vocabulary tests each Friday.

Books on the desktop might have papers (and answers) peeking out. And it became all too obvious they did when kids at surrounding desks craned to read these cheat sheets. Enid, a bright, energetic eighth grader who could—when there were no other options—commit the definitions to memory, preferred to write the answers on a sheet of paper and put it on the floor next to her desk. But she wasn't farsighted enough to see it without doubling over with her head far below the desktop, an immediate red flag for me as a teacher. Or she might put the definitions on the piece of paper taped to the inside of her forearm. But the pushed-up sleeve of her maroon, school-uniform sweater was a giveaway. So was the bright white paper against her dark brown skin.

Alfred, the smiling, well-mannered recent African immigrant who couldn't read, was unabashed about pulling answers off his neighbors' papers. On Fridays (quiz days), he apparently believed his assigned seat was precisely on top of Santos, the class wizard, who actually studied and had a 100+ average. Like other kids, Alfred tried handing in a prewritten answer sheet with the week's vocabulary words and definitions numbered 1 to 10 in the order they were given on Monday.

"But the test wasn't given in that order," I said, suggesting I was on to the con.

"Really?" the typical perpetrator would say. "The order is wrong, but the answers are right. Right?"

Faux surprise was every kid's response to getting caught cheating. In fact, "*What happened?*"—delivered in a shocked tone that was to be interpreted as "I didn't do anything, it must've occurred by itself"—was the usual response to being caught doing anything from talking to cheating to tossing a fellow student over a row of desks. For these students, there was no shame in being caught cheating. And it created virtually no reaction from the rest of the class, which only reinforced their nonchalance about doing it. One student accusing another of farting caused a whooping, hollering uproar, but Mr. Owens pulling your paper away and saying, "You're getting a zero on today's test," was barely worth a shrug.[*]

For many students, tests were, at best, a game, a distraction from class. At worst, they were wasted time to stare off into space and do nothing. Nothing at all. The real problem quickly became apparent. Despite a steady stream of state, city, school, and class tests, the kids never saw much in the way of consequences in school, whether they did well, did poorly, or did nothing at all. Those who constantly misbehaved in class didn't pay for it so, the kids' thinking went, why should a student who is actually trying (albeit by dishonesty) to get a better grade be severely punished? And, as we'll see, it was also in the teacher's best interest to not hand out too many zeros for cheating for fear of wrecking the class "passing rate."

Latinate's calendar of tests—performance indicators—was jam-packed and started immediately with the school year. Each teacher received six pages of test and grading schedules along with a seventeen-page *Test Administration Handbook* from the city that was an explosion of bright-pink highlighting, courtesy of Ms. P's secretary. While I was overwhelmed just by the number of English assessments I had to administer for them, the students had tests in every academic subject.

---

[*]Students and teachers nationwide report student cheating across the economic and academic spectrum. In a 2010 ABC NEWS poll of high school students aged fifteen to seventeen, 36 percent admitted to having cheated, and seven in ten said they had friends who cheat.

As the 2012 school year ended, New York City's highly prestigious Stuyvesant High School was embroiled in a cheating scandal that involved upwards of eighty students and cell-phone text messages. According to a June 27, 2012, article in the *Wall Street Journal,* the editor of the school newspaper reported that a recent survey of students showed "rampant" cheating.

City, state, and class tests aside, Latinate also had its own quarterly exams in each subject. These were to be used to "not only chart our students' growth, but also…to inform our instruction" (the same language used by Tennessee and other value-added adherents). That is, this additional data would help teachers determine how much our students knew and if what we were teaching was sinking in. As if homework, classwork, exit slips, quizzes, writing assignments, and frequency of absences weren't enough to help us shape our day-to-day lessons, we needed *data* so we could chart, plot, and otherwise graphically represent the results of our teaching.

Early September found me reading a nonfiction text to the kids and having them answer multiple-choice questions. I would then grade those exams ("Baseline") and administer the exact same exam (yes, the same questions) three more times during the year ("Interim 1," "Interim 2," and "Endline") to watch their progress soar. From the start—I mean "Baseline"—it was clear that we had no place to go but up. The test supplied by Ms. P involved a piece on early immigration to New York and some straightforward questions. Typical social-studies textbook stuff. As instructed, I read it aloud slowly twice while the kids had the multiple-choice questions in front of them.

The results? Yikes! Had anyone been listening? Did anybody care? Some kids didn't even hand in an answer sheet. Or an answer sheet with any answers. Many of those who did fill out the paper scored below 40 percent. Very few got everything right.

Then I dutifully filled in the Excel spreadsheet for my 125 students. It had these headings: Baseline…Interim 1…Difference… Interim 2…Difference…Endline…Final Difference. We were supposed to fill it out for each student six times a year. We were not, however, allowed to record the actual score the student earned on the test if it was below 55. So a 40 was a 55. Even a zero was 55.

At Latinate, as well as throughout the New York City system, the minimum grade any student could get was 55. The idea is to make failure quite difficult to achieve. So even if a kid spent the test period—or *every* period—wadding up bits of paper in his mouth and fast-balling them at his peers while muttering the words "Fuck you!" and handed in an answer sheet that was blank except for his name, his score would be no lower than 55. Failing, but still within striking distance of a passing 65. And pretty much guaranteed to pass if the teacher adhered to Ms. P's non-negotiable policy that was imparted at the orientation in August:

> We must ensure that every failing mark for each marking period is reversed to a passing mark via make-up work (independent study, packets, etc.) for the students in our advisory groups.

Take, for instance, Africah's sometime boyfriend, Santiago. He rarely came to class. He never did classwork, homework, or any sort of work, though he often could sit quietly. The lowest grade he could receive on his report card was 55. But if I didn't ensure that he did make-up work to pass, I wasn't doing my job.

A failing grade for Santiago could bite me in other ways, too. With report cards coming six times every school year, a half-dozen grades of 55 would fail him for the year. And a few students like Santiago could sink a teacher like me by bringing down the overall passing rate of my class.

Every one of my classes had kids who did nothing. Ms. P assigned several simultaneous ninth, tenth, and eleventh graders such as Shaneblane to even my best ninth-grade classes. The idea was "credit recovery"—giving these kids another (and often another and another) shot at getting credit for a class they had failed previously. Most of these students were determined to do even less work and pay less attention than they had in earlier incarnations of the course, and I found it impossible to engage them in many of my lessons.

To give them something to do—and keep them from disrupting the class—I bought a bunch of word-search books at a dollar store and tore out pages that I gave to the do-nothing kids on a daily basis. This was work they would do. They enjoyed it. And if it exposed them to new words, so much the better. But when the lead teacher saw this, her eyes got wide and she said to never give the kids puzzles or word searches; it's not academic work.

"But they won't do anything else…" I cut myself off. "Okay. No more puzzles or word searches."

Ms. P required that we administer a test at least every other week, and the assistant principal asked that I present one test a week that was in the same format as the state Regents Exam to prepare the students for that. On top of this, I was to put into the SnapGrades online grading system scores for homework, classwork, notebook, and core values (academic excellence, community citizenship, unity of being, reflective living, self-determination, compassion, and integrity). Along with attendance, it worked out to more than 2,000 entries per week…if I kept up with the data input. But I could barely find the time to accurately gather so much data, let alone manually input all of it.

In all, the evaluation system for the kids was a lot like Ms. P's sixty-six-point teacher evaluation system—there were so many elements and so many variables and so many subjective grades that anything good or bad could be "proven." And it could be "proven" with the weight of online reporting systems, spreadsheets, and other "data." The trouble was, some of the kids had no positive data at all. No work, no quizzes, not much of anything except maybe showing up.

"If a child attends class at least twice a week, you should be able to have an impact," the assistant principal told the teachers at a staff meeting. Ms. P stood nearby, nodding in affirmation with a deep, serious scowl. Nobody said a word. We knew better than to challenge this assertion and suggest it was a delusional fantasy. The administrators would have immediately countered that if a kid who *ever* came to class was failing, it was still simply because the teacher was ineffective. So at report-card time, I had more than a dozen students with averages at or close to single digits. They were instantly boosted to 55.

But that wasn't enough. In order for me to be considered an effective teacher, at least 80 percent of my students had to pass. That meant a grade of 65. If less than 80 percent of any class was passing, the city's Department of Education might see the data as an indication of not only an ineffective teacher, but also of an ineffective school. And with the administration of these small schools so intimately intertwined with the principal's visionary leadership, it might signal an ineffective principal. Which of course, was a near-impossibility, a virtual oxymoron in the principal-centric system.

At Latinate, any teacher who failed more than 20 percent of a class had to immediately come up with an action plan to remedy the situation by the next marking period. The school's teacher's handbook had a couple of pages of suitable action-plan actions:

- Create a chart of missing work on the wall.
- Confer with students, parents, guidance counselors, and other teachers.

- Celebrate student work on the wall; call or email parent whenever a child achieves something notable.
- Pull students out during lunch and tutor.
- Provide parents with a weekly printout of SnapGrades, and request that parents sign the printout or give you a call to confirm receipt.
- Contact parent to come to school after a child misses three homework submissions.
- Provide students with differentiated materials, quizzes, tests, etc.
- Appoint peer tutors.
- Organize after-school study hall with teacher and parent volunteers to oversee students completing homework.
- Give students a lot of work so that even if they complete only half of it, there is still a basis for a passing grade.

...And so on. I would have happily set to work on these steps if anyone honestly believed they would get results. These are all reasonable approaches for students who are trying and not quite making it. But for Shaneblane, Santiago, Natasha and her posse, and a dozen others who did nothing? C'mon. It was laughable. Instead, the best action-plan advice I received was from another teacher at Latinate:

"Don't fail more than 20 percent of the class," the teacher said. "Do the math."

"Wow!" I said. "I have never seen any organization where corruption was encouraged at such a low level."

My colleague just shrugged. I realized I was working in the education equivalent of a Mexican police department—corruption throughout the ranks.

With this advice in mind, in the first marking period, at least

80 percent of all the students in every class I taught passed. And the failures—though many deserved zeros—received no lower than 55. Thanks to six marking periods, even a kid with a couple of 55s could—with a 70 or two thrown in, as well as some creative rounding—pass for the year.

For me, it was a distasteful exercise in statistics. Though I never heard it discussed openly, I'm sure that "do-the-math" grading is a far more standard operating procedure across the public school system. It could be argued that a teacher is simply grading on a curve, and curving the class grades so that 80 percent pass. Unfortunately, that means students who aren't really being students at all, but merely using the school as a waiting room for either graduation or adulthood, will pass…or it's the teacher's fault.

I felt a tinge of that *"Run away! Really, run away!"* panic as I saw how quickly my mission of helping kids had been transformed into the role of an accomplice in a crazy and corrupt system bent on achieving statistical results, rather than helping students.

———————

The Scholarship Reports prepared on the Department of Education computers showed an impressive amount of data, with passing rates carried to the second decimal point. The idea is that this kind of number-crunching indicates a very effective educational system. And my 81.82 percent pass rate even may have signaled the makings of an effective pedagogue. In fact, soon after the first marking period I received a commendation, a letter from the assistant principal congratulating me for passing enough students to keep the school in the Department of Education's "safe harbor." It was the only positive material I can recall that may have made its way to my personnel file.

I cringed when I read the letter. I wasn't being commended for my teaching, but for my *data*. Data that I'd felt I had to create—I mean, report. And the administration made it fairly clear to me that I had better make sure that I continued to produce a safe-harbor passing rate of 80+ percent. Falling short of that would mean implementing yet another action plan that involved so much additional (and fruitless) work that it would only drain more from my efforts to help the kids. Further, just as exceeding the safe-harbor figure earned me a commendation in my personnel file, falling short of the rate no doubt would have led to a rebuke and absolutely, positively ensured my dismissal at the end of the school year.

I long suspected, however, that school administrations didn't rely solely on the teachers to skew the data, and various conversations I overheard at Latinate, as well as media reports, pointed toward widespread, systemic manipulation of the numbers. Thus, when news of Atlanta's huge cheating scandal broke in early 2010, implicating administrators far above the classroom level, I was certain that this sort of thing was not confined to just 191 schools in Georgia.

It was the same sort of corruption issue that led to the dismissal of Eileen Scotto, the seemingly kind-hearted principal I mentioned earlier, who I had hoped would hire me at the High School for Artistic Trades. In 2012, after a seventeen-month investigation, the DOE issued a 110-page report identifying testing fraud and transcript tampering at Scotto's school. Under the principal's direction, data had been adjusted to keep the passing rate at 97 percent and the attendance rate similarly high, said the report.

Scotto's data had boosted her school to the top of the city ratings. One year, the school was celebrated as the best high school in New York City, "proving" that charter-style schools are better. And unlike the warm person I met, Scotto was a vindictive tyrant, some teachers reported. "She is an evil person," one staffer told the *New York Post*. It made me realize that perhaps, even there, I had dodged a bullet. And more than anything, I realized that massaged, manipulated, and invented data was part of an even wider systemic failure in education evaluation.

However, the strongest indication—and vindication—came almost immediately after the article on my experiences at Latinate appeared on Salon.com. Suddenly, the New York media was buzzing with news of Ms. P and the assistant principal being booted amid allegations of cooking the academic books. According to the *New York Post*, the pair had boosted "graduation numbers by crediting students for courses they never took."

Kids retaking a class they had already taken would earn credit for a class they needed to graduate. The allegations were saying, in other words, that a kid taking eighth- or ninth-grade English for the second or third time (as nearly a dozen of my students were) earned credit for taking tenth-, eleventh-, or twelfth-grade English or some other required course. That kind of corrupt "credit recovery" would give these kids a high school diploma.

Media reports said that Ms. P vociferously denied the allegations, but that statements made by the assistant principal, as well as an email trail, pointed to the principal's knowledge—and even masterminding—of the scheme.

I laughed out loud and jumped up from my computer, doing a little NFL-style touchdown dance when I read the news that both of them were—as the *New York Post* put it—"yanked from the school." I was delighted to see that the assistant principal had finally turned on his merciless, U-bestowing master. Now, he was cooperating with the authorities.

Ms. Lyons called in giddy excitement. Mr. Bookbinder spoke at length about how happy he was. Several of my former colleagues thanked me for writing the article that made the DOE act. I'm not taking credit, though the timing suggests my piece on Salon.com helped trigger city officials to confront Ms. P and the assistant principal when they did.

So much for appearances.

So much for data.

So much for visionary leadership.

Voices of Teachers around the Country

Mrs. Chili, English Teacher, New England

I found myself engaged—wholly and enthusiastically and not altogether pleasantly—in a conversation about failing students with my director the other day.

We're at fourth-quarter progress reports, and the reports across the board aren't very good. We teachers each have a significant number of students failing our classes. This failure isn't due to overly rigorous material or an accelerated pace or an unreasonable expectation for our students; this failure is due almost entirely to the fact that the kids simply aren't doing what we're asking of them. Not that they *can't*, but that they're choosing not to.

My argument is that we, as teachers, can't be held accountable for that kind of attitude from the students. We're doing our jobs, and if the kids who *are* doing the work are any indication, we're doing our jobs well. The problem is that some students simply aren't willing to play along with us, and as a result of failing to produce work (in one case, a student turned in *one* assignment out of twenty), they're failing the classes.

My director was looking at it from an administrative standpoint—she has to be concerned with numbers and percentages and how all of this looks to the Department of Education, and I get that—and argued that we had to "meet the students where they are."

That, to me, says that she's asking us to alter our curriculum, change our policies, and essentially allow the inmates to run the asylum to make sure we pass "enough" students.

Mrs. Chili has taken a year off from teaching to pursue a Certificate in Advanced Graduate Studies in Adolescent Development. She blogs at http://teacherseducation.word press.com.

WHAT I LEARNED

[M]ost Americans are unaware that children have no constitutional protection where equality of education is at stake. The notion that education is not a protected right under the U.S. Constitution comes as a surprise to the majority of citizens...

—Jonathan Kozol, *The Shame of the Nation: The Restoration of Apartheid Schooling in America*, 2005

DURING MY TIME AT Latinate Institute, I learned many things. For example, "dumb tight" means "very much." And "O.D." means "to the furthest extent."

I knew that I loved working with kids, and I came to see how O.D. dumb tight I relished the challenges and occasional victories of teaching them. And, for all their tough talk and hardass posing, my fellow teachers did, too.

More importantly, however, my time in the South Bronx taught me that American education is in big trouble. The bad-teacher witch hunt and current definition of school reform are having a long-term, unproductive effect on so many truly needy children—children who could succeed and deserve to succeed. In that regard, here are ten crucial lessons for how to fix the problems plaguing our educational system.

Lesson 1: The problem isn't bad teachers.

The March 5, 2010 cover of *Newsweek* spoke for popular sentiment when it declared, "The Key to Saving American Education: We Must Fire Bad Teachers."

If only it were as simple as quantifying who is a good teacher, who is a bad teacher, and fixing or booting the bad ones. But it's not.

We talk about bad teachers, but all too often we mean all teachers. As *The New Yorker*'s Rebecca Mead wrote in September 2012, "A certain casual demonization of teachers has become sufficiently culturally prevalent that it passes for uncontroversial." In the eyes of the public, bad teachers have become what welfare queens were in the 1970s—layabouts eating richly from the public trough, enjoying lavish pensions, two-month-long summer vacations, and comfortable tenure packages—and they must be rooted out and punished. The quickest route to this is to break the unions that protect all of these supposedly ineffective educators.

Of course, the truth is far from the image. The teachers I worked with at Latinate were excellent. Exceptional. I would want them to teach my daughter. The problem was everything around them—from the principal's nutty expectations to the poor, even nonexistent facilities to the lack of people and programs to help the many troubled, needy students. And it's much the same around the country. Teachers are being maligned despite their commitment. To be a teacher today requires a thick skin and incurable idealism, regardless of the school situation. Those who enter and remain in this field amid the budget-squeezed cutbacks, data-driven accountability, and highly structured teaching are in it because it's a calling. Not because it's cushy.

The Bill & Melinda Gates Foundation constantly says that teacher effectiveness is the Number 1 factor in student achievement. This gives the impression that a student's personality, economic situation, family life, neighborhood, nutrition, health, social abilities, psychological health, prior education or language skills, and a range of other issues outside of the school's—let alone the teacher's—control are not nearly as important as how a teacher operates the Smart Board for forty-six minutes 182 days each year.

That simply isn't true. Teachers can make a difference—a huge difference—in a kid's life and education, but it's ridiculous to suggest that teaching, not poverty, is holding kids back. As Daniel T. Willingham, a professor of cognitive psychology at the University of Virginia, noted in the article "Why Does Family Wealth Affect Learning?" in the Spring 2012 issue of *American Educator*:

> [C]hildren from poorer homes are subject to chronic stress, which research from the last ten years has shown is more destructive to learning than was previously guessed.... [O]n average, kids from wealthy families do significantly better than kids from poor families. Household wealth is associated with IQ and school achievement, and that phenomenon is observed to varying degrees throughout the world.... [W]e see associations with wealth in more basic academic skills like reading achievement and math achievement. And the association with wealth is still observed if we examine even more basic cognitive processes such as phonological awareness, or the amount of information the child can

keep in working memory...or to the extent to which the
child can regulate his emotions and thought processes.

Clearly, the real issue is that everything from reading to math
comprehension to behavior has a biological root in poverty and
the environments children grow up in. Not inadequate teaching. I
have noticed that in well-funded public school systems—like the
one my daughter is fortunate to attend in suburban Long Island—
the hot-button issues are not bad teachers and data signifying student achievement. Parents complain loudly and powerfully about
how a particular teacher is dealing with their particular child, but
overall school reform? Not here. In these pockets of privilege, the
big problems are the problems that come with money—drug and
alcohol abuse, crashes in expensive cars, and worries about which
top-tier college the kids will attend.

There is no way around that. Clubs, after-school activities,
and a full range of cultural, athletic, and recreational activities fill
out the school day in wealthy communities and supplement the
school year. These areas are dense with pediatricians, psycholo-
gists, nutritionists, coaches, and well-trained tutors, all of whom
can help students advance and improve their education and
healthy development. Most parents are involved, care about, and
spend heavily—sometimes insanely—on their children's education. These kids get the whole package—what social service types
call "wrap-around services"—that help them with the sound body
and sound mind needed to learn and achieve. If poor kids had
the same family involvement as well as community services and
opportunities, they, too, could do far better.

Rather than point fingers and assign blame, America must
address the many real problems we face. In some areas, officials
point to bad teachers, though tight budgets are the real problem.

In others, the real issue is unrealistic expectations. Rather than say, "No, this school can't do more with less," teachers are labeled as roadblocks to efficiency. But such middle-class matters aside, poverty—and all of the issues associated with it—is the leading cause of America's educational problems. The problem is not the teachers who are trying to save these children. Until we are willing to face the issues associated with wealth disparity in this country, we aren't honestly looking for answers.

Lesson 2: Everyone is cheating.

The kids, the teachers, and the administrators in the American public school system are awash in a sea of corruption. It can be labeled with softer euphemisms, but it's still cheating and lying.

The kids are cheating because it's a lot easier—and more fun—than studying. They also are cheating because they have learned that it is an effective solution to the problem of schoolwork. And it is widespread. In an article published September 25, 2012, ethics researcher Michael Josephson told the *New York Times* that his 2010 survey of 40,000 high school students found that 59 percent admitted cheating on a test during the previous year, with one-third saying they had used the Internet to plagiarize. Perhaps most telling of all, a quarter of the respondents admitted lying on Josephson's survey.

The adults can grouse, scold, and take limited disciplinary actions. But really serious enforcement—such as failing, leaving back, and expelling—is rare. Even in the nationally reported cheating scandal at New York City's prestigious Stuyvesant High School in 2012, the most severe punishments were ten-day suspensions.

For teachers and administrators at all levels across the country, reliance on student "data" has created intense pressure to prove effectiveness and progress. And, of course, an increasing number of evaluation systems use student test data as a factor in rating teachers—usually, scores of their students on state standardized tests. Thus, in most schools, it's not in the teachers' or administrators' best interest to fail students for cheating, since it impacts their data by lowering the "passing rate."

America's education-data obsession went into overdrive when President George W. Bush signed the No Child Left Behind Act into law in 2002. The legislation was seen as a positive step by people of various stripes, and even Bush's political antipode Ted Kennedy praised the approach.

The idea behind No Child Left Behind was to make sure that students prove their achievement by passing state-wide standardized tests. In schools with a large number of kids from low-income families, each year's grade-level test scores had to exceed the previous year's.

Schools that didn't improve year over year for two years in a row were labeled "in need of improvement" and required to develop a two-year improvement plan. Students also were allowed to transfer out of the school to attend a "better" school. Failure to hit the test target on a third year required the school to provide tutoring and other catch-up services. A fourth year of insufficient progress meant "corrective action" such as replacing the staff and longer school days. By year five, if failure continued, plans were drawn up to restructure the school if there wasn't enough improvement by the end of year six. And that could mean closing the school, turning it into a charter school, or even a state takeover.

At the same time, the state was to ensure that all students were taught by "highly qualified" teachers. How to determine that standard was left up to each state. Problems became evident right away. While the goal was student improvement, No Child Left

Behind gave the impression that American education was failing because someone was to blame. And now there was data to prove it. The law ended up putting federal muscle behind a punitive education system that advocated "get results or else."

Since then, education chancellors, superintendents, and principals around the country have used those very words to put their teachers on notice. While the federal law did not specify using test data to rate individual teachers—just the particular school—many school districts crunched the numbers down to the classroom level to determine whether or not they employed "highly qualified" teachers. That made it so easy to assign the blame for failure.

But even with threats, Unsatisfactory ratings, and firings, the data still didn't get where No Child Left Behind demanded it be. By the act's tenth anniversary, all but a handful of states had applied for a waiver of 100 percent compliance with the law's test-score requirements.

Nonetheless, the frenzy for data as a marker of success or failure had taken hold, and there have been no waivers from the widespread attitude of "get results or else." The consequence is that educators across America have turned into the Bernie Madoffs of test scores. Erasures and re-coding of answer sheets on state tests have been suspected in dozens of large school districts. The statistical improbability of so many kids changing their minds on answers and getting passing grades has impressed mathematicians. So have the year-to-year upswings in test scores.

Following a major cheating scandal in Atlanta's public schools, the *Atlanta Journal-Constitution*'s 2012 investigation, "Cheating Our Children," presented the frightening evidence. In the first part of the series, published March 25, 2012, the newspaper reported uncovering "suspicious test scores in roughly 200 school districts" around the country. The analysis of test results for 69,000 public schools "found high concentrations of suspect math or reading scores in school systems from coast to coast…. Some of the most persistently suspicious test scores nationwide…occurred in districts renowned for cutting-edge reforms…. State investigators later confirmed scores that year were widely manipulated by educators who assisted students improperly and outright changed tens of thousands of their answers on state tests."

An April 30, 2012, follow-up article by Alan Judd, John Perry, and Heather Vogell suggests there's little urgency in rooting out this sort of data corruption:

> In the spring of 2008, students at a Mobile, Ala., middle school discovered something weird on their yearly achievement tests: someone, somehow, had changed their answers. But when their teacher alerted the principal, he suggested she proceed with caution.
>
> "Sleep on it," the principal said.
>
> When the teacher reported the apparent cheating to Alabama's state education department, it ordered a thorough investigation of Scarborough Middle School. But not too thorough. Computer analyses that might detect organized tampering, the state superintendent of education says, would have amounted to a "witch hunt."
>
> The Mobile episode, detailed in interviews and public records, illustrates the haphazard manner in which many states and school districts handle reports of cheating on high-stakes achievement tests, The Atlanta Journal-Constitution has found. Officials often minimize such allegations, treating them as mere aberrations: one-time occurrences best dealt with in isolation.

An analysis of 2009 New York State Regents Examination scores by the *Wall Street Journal* showed a bulge in the number of students who received a 65, the minimum passing grade. As *Journal* reporters Barbara Martinez and Tom McGinty put it in an article published on February 2, 2011:

> Experts on testing and statistics said the results suggested widespread score inflation. For the 2009 U.S. History and Government Regents, for example, New York students were fourteen times more likely to get a 65 than one point lower.

As a result, the state banned administrators and teachers from grading their own students' Regents Exams. We are lying if we deny that data manipulation is now so widespread in American education that it's systemic.

Data is a key element in President Barack Obama's Race to the Top, which got under way in early 2010 and rewards states with federal money for innovations such as using student test results to measure teachers and allowing students from low-performing schools to go to charter schools. While No Child Left Behind used test data to rank only schools, Race to the Top further encourages data-backed teacher evaluations. The results are not only more finger-pointing, but also poor management, says Harry Frank, an expert on testing and measurement and emeritus professor of psychology at the University of Michigan.

In a letter posted July 17, 2012 on education historian Diane Ravitch's blog, Dr. Frank says, "The first principle is that no assessment can be used at the same time for both counseling and for administrative decisions (retention, increment, tenure, promotion).... [A]ll this does is promote cheating and teaching to the exam…. This principle is so basic that it's often covered in the very first chapter of introductory texts on workplace performance evaluation."

Another option is to lower the bar so you get the data you need. Teachers have done it; even states have done it. You can call it "differentiated instruction," but coloring is still coloring. Especially when high school kids are coloring. Lower standards may not have the ring of perjury, though this is cheating nonetheless, since it cheats the kids out of the education they need, and the education that they and their parents believe they are receiving.

The answer, I believe, is not a data system that is more immune to manipulation. Rather, we should rely less on data and seek a broader way to evaluate student learning. Perhaps, for instance, there should be an annual exam of *everything* an eighth grader should know in a variety of topics. The material could be so wide-ranging that there's no way to narrowly teach to the test and make school simply a test-prep factory. This exam could demonstrate much more clearly than today's system what an individual student knows and still needs to learn. Not punitive, but truly diagnostic.

While it may seem radical, this approach would be much like the schools most Americans attended decades ago. Imagine students learning music and art, running for student government, playing volleyball, and doing much more than just cramming for state tests on the "core" subjects of math and English. Yes, there's a slim possibility we could end up with a nation full of *Jeopardy!* champions, but at least we'd be far better off than we are today.

Lesson 3: The data panic hits poor kids hardest.

The high-stakes tests and data-intensive approach to learning were supposed to help students in the most underserved, least-funded areas: demand results and get them by enforcing strict tests. But from what I can see, it has backfired.

The tests required by No Child Left Behind are progressive. That is, each year they build on the skills of the previous years. On one level it makes sense. But what if a kid isn't up to speed to start with? And what if the kid isn't gaining ground as fast as the tests progress? And what if the kid is among the many, many students in poor areas who fit this profile, not because they aren't bright, but because poverty, family situations, lack of health and psychological care, as well as poor nutrition, have given them a slow start and have made catch-up tougher?

In that case, the teachers must help the kids cram for the state test. Constantly review the material that will be asked and practice the techniques of test-taking. "Our kids don't know how to take tests," the lead teacher told me. "We have to give them a lot of practice in taking tests."

And we did. Weekly, at least. Class time devoted to filling in dots with a #2 pencil is time you can't spend reading, writing, and thinking. From what I can see, high-needs schools are increasingly becoming test-prep factories for those who can pass. For those who can't pass, there's always data manipulation.

With schools, administrators, and teachers punished for data that doesn't make the grade (pun intentional), the need to meet the standards is *desperate*. The strictures of No Child Left Behind may be waived, but no teacher or administrator can forget a federal mandate that schools failing to meet standards year after year lose funding, lose students (usually the best ones), and ultimately lose their right to survive.

Anyone who isn't looking for someone to blame for America's education problems would understand that poor-performing schools typically need more resources, not punishment and cuts.

It's a tough message to hear in today's tight economy, but high-needs schools are called that for a reason, and it's time we started helping them, not hurting.

Lesson 4: We want to believe in miracles, but we have to create them.

Visionary leaders who get results by being as inspiring and courageous as they are demanding. Brilliant, energetic, newly minted teachers who can turn around classes and change lives before the marking period is over. Old-timers who pack it in and move on when they discover that everything they have done for decades is completely wrong, and they realize they can never match the passion, the commitment, and sheer wonderfulness of reformers. And, of course, the kids, giddy with the excitement of learning, plead to touch the hem of the reformers' cloaks, as each child is scooped up for the incoming class of an Ivy League university. Best of all, our kids receive this awesome education at a far lower cost than today.

These are all elements of the mantra of school-reform advocates, which is that education isn't about money. It's about passion, commitment, new blood, leadership, and great ideas. When those ingredients finally make their way to a school, miracles happen.

If only it were that simple. Unfortunately for the promoters of school reform, and for the rest of us, it's not. I have come to see that there are no new ideas in education. New technology, yes. But fundamental approaches to instruction and learning? Not that I can see. Rather, we encounter old ideas that are repackaged, rejiggered, and re-jargoned as today's great breakthroughs. Sorry, we can't bully our way to educational success, and we can't overlook the fact that education is about developing individuals. Unfortunately, that takes time, trained people, and lots of money.

We prefer, instead, to believe in miracles and instant results. Meanwhile, the kids at Latinate—and millions just like them—await a miracle to instantly transform their lives and repair this broken system.

Perhaps the greatest miracle of all would be America recognizing that saving our educational system will be a long-term, big-budget project, similar to the way we tend to look at things like wars. I believe it is essential for America to commit to overhauling our schools and investing in both infrastructure and personnel. It might be slower and messier than a miracle, but it will work.

If we don't take that bold step and instead continue looking for miracles, America will continue to fail so many of our children. When our country discovers that visionary leadership with strong, data-backed management isn't the miracle we need, we will fall prey to the next miracle. That, no doubt, will be the digital teacher—a tablet or computer-style contraption loaded with books, lessons, videos, tests, and other teaching tools that promises to do everything a teacher can do and more. Only do it better and less expensively.

Lesson 5: There is no cheap solution.

It is time for America to decide: do we really believe what we are saying about ensuring that every kid gets a globally competitive education? Even kids who are capable but first must overcome serious handicaps, such as health or emotional issues; not speaking, reading, or writing English; or coming from poor and troubled homes? Even kids who don't seem to want that education?

If we truly mean it, we will have to be prepared to pay. I saw that getting kids like Alfred, the cheerful African immigrant who couldn't read, and the snarling, emotionally unsettled Natasha to the point where they could legitimately graduate from high school would be very expensive. Getting Africah, my sixteen-year-old eighth grader, through middle school as well as high school might be the educational equivalent of putting a man on the moon. Far more costly than putting the bright, motivated Santos, the already well-prepared Ron, the eager-to-succeed Mark, and the bright (though sometimes cheating) Enid on the fast track to college and academic success.

As a nation, we are asking a huge amount from our schools. Not only that we build a workforce that is second to none in the world, but also that *every* child—regardless of disability, inability, or outright refusal—get a full education. Considering that we are talking about kids from coast to coast and from conditions ranging from the South Bronx to Beverly Hills, that is a staggeringly ambitious project. Wonderfully altruistic. But America must understand what it is asking and be realistic about what it costs to do this.

If we are not willing to pay, we *will* have to leave some children behind. As it stands, many are being left behind. We, as a culture, however, aren't willing to admit it.

Lesson 6: First-year teachers need a lot of support.

Beginners are not necessarily bad teachers. But they need help. Teaching is a skill, craft, and art that is learned and perfected over time. The first skill a teacher must acquire is getting the kids to sit down and do something resembling schoolwork. That's classroom management. In a school such as Latinate, with Ms. P's expectation that the scholars study silently in the cathedral of learning, the importance of classroom management can't be overstated. While schools nationwide may not set the bar as high, classroom management is a challenge (to put it mildly) for almost all first-year teachers.

The wry conventional wisdom says that teachers everywhere spend their first year crying. Or at least under a great deal of stress. The 2011 edition of the annual publication *Tomorrow's Teachers* from the National Education Association has a piece by Mary Ellen Flannery called "Stress!"

> [T]he high-stakes stress of a first-year teacher is a whole new experience.
>
> The nightmares: I was naked in front of the class!
>
> The headaches: I collapsed into bed at 6 p.m.
>
> The weight-gain: Good-bye, perfect jeans.
>
> It's not unusual for first-year teachers to actually make themselves sick from stress and long hours. Their classroom lights are still burning at 9 p.m., as they work on the next day's activities, and their eyes are still shining at 3 a.m., as they run through state standards in their mind.

There's much truth to that. Not only is the workload taxing, but it's also terribly frustrating to not be able to implement your lessons and demonstrate your passion and commitment amid the chaos of sugar-fueled eighth graders. Also, while kids respond to passion and enthusiasm, their response is not always quiet or orderly.

For most teachers, achieving reasonable classroom management skills—especially in a high-needs school—takes at least a couple of years.

Ms. Lyons, the science teacher who was a veteran of Bronx middle schools, was a master of these skills. Like the other experienced pros I worked with, Ms. Lyons had the skills to keep the kids quiet and she understood how much—actually, *how little*—the average class could master in a day, week, or grading period. In teaching, as in show business or my long-time career, magazine publishing, success comes with knowing your audience. Knowing your audience on a visceral level comes only through experience.

That our most needy schools and our most needy students are taught by so many beginner teachers is not a positive for their education. Neither is the constant turnover of teachers.* A steady stream of energetic, fresh faces appeals to those who see education through the lens of Hollywood fantasy. ("My uncle has a barn! Let's put on a show!") Low-cost beginners also appeal to principals with bottom-line budget responsibility. But even with passion and good intentions, new teachers who are caught in a system where they come and go like educational migrant workers are no match for stable, experienced teachers when it comes to student achievement.

I believe that America should return to the notion of teaching as a long-term career and recognize that the first few years really are an apprenticeship, and as such, new teachers should be matched with veteran teachers who are eager and able to serve as mentor-coaches. These roles and relationships must be totally separate from evaluation and personnel (firing) decisions. This approach would help cut the sense of being overwhelmed that

---

*A 2011 report on 600,000 elementary school kids in New York City by the National Bureau of Economic Research (http://www.nber.org/papers/w17176) shows that classes with high teacher turnover had lower scores in both English and math. The detrimental effects of teachers in revolving door positions were especially acute in low-performing schools with large proportions of black students, said the report. Why would middle schools and high schools be any different?

new teachers feel while improving their skills, which would benefit their students more quickly. But as the next lesson shows, even that's not enough.

Lesson 7: America needs better teacher training. And much more special-ed training.

To teach in today's increasingly test-oriented schools with their strictly choreographed instruction, how much English do you really have to know? Or math? Or science? Or anything else except the "best practices" that foster student achievement (as demonstrated by high standardized-test scores)? A love of the subject matter and a deep knowledge of it are so old school. That's a shame.

At *all* schools, getting the students to sit down, do the work, and learn something is very, very important. It is a crucial step toward then getting them to really love the subject and learn more deeply.

The nuts and bolts of classroom management and instruction are essential to a teacher's success, yet from what I could see, the people in teacher training and licensing haven't gotten that message.

Courses with names such as "Effective Urban Schools," "Child and Adolescent Development," "Teaching and Learning," "Exceptionalities: Individualizing Learning," and "Teaching Diverse Learners" are a good start. But they are hardly enough. In New York State, all you need to begin a teaching career are a bachelor's degree in just about anything as well as a handful of education courses and some time spent observing another pedagogue at work. Becoming a principal in the New York City system doesn't take much more, especially at the new small schools such as Latinate. An even quicker route to a full-time job is to join the city's Teaching Fellows, which requires only a college degree and a summer of pre-service training.

Nationally, the path to teaching has been similarly short-ened for those headed to high-needs schools. Most famously, Teach for America places more than 5,000 brand-new teachers around the country each year. These recent college grads agree to a two-year commitment and undergo a stunningly brief five-week training program that involves classwork and teaching summer-school students before they are placed in front of their students.

The master's of teaching program at Empire State College and Latinate each provided mentoring and coaching for me. But this assistance was an educational Tower of Babel, with conflicting instructions and no coordination. Even before Ms. P and her posse decided to use the mentoring system to certify me as a bad teacher, I was, like most new teachers, dazed and confused by what passed for support.* I sought advice from Bronx-tested colleagues such as Ms. Lyons, but even advice from straight-talking pros wasn't enough for me to meet Ms. P's expectations, especially with special-needs students, whom a new teacher like me would never have the qualifications or experience to teach fresh from school.

My eighth-period eighth-grade class had many kids with learning disabilities, behavioral problems, and other issues that required a skilled special-ed teacher. But Ms. Perker, the freshly minted special-ed teacher assigned to the class, was rarely in the room since her superiors saw other duties as more pressing. My

---

*A survey of 167 new math teachers in New York City's Teaching Fellows program published in the June 2011 issue of the journal *Education and Urban Society* found 38 percent reporting they didn't receive the professional guidance required by the city and state. More than three-quarters of these classroom novices told researchers that they had built their own informal support networks.

special-ed training? One class in graduate school and, at Latinate, these instructions:

"Don't yell," the assistant principal told me. "And never say 'Shut up!' It's considered offensive to these kids. Like using 'nigger.'"

More than 12 percent of America's elementary and secondary students have an individualized education program, according to a September 2001 report from the National Center for Education Statistics (http://nces.ed.gov/pubs2001/overview/table10.asp). These special-ed plans are for kids with a range of learning and behavior challenges, as well as immigrants who are learning English. While the 2001 number is high, there's no doubt that current numbers are higher. And certainly higher still in areas like the South Bronx, with its high immigrant population. Yet visionary leaders such as Ms. P pretend these numbers aren't high, tossing general-education teachers in front of what are, in effect, special-ed classes and demanding "Amazing!" results.

From what I could see, a lot of the work in the South Bronx is in special education. Even among the mainstream kids. They have been so influenced by their out-of-control classmates that many truly don't know how to behave or concentrate. The policy of putting special-needs students in mainstream classes as much as possible is founded on good intentions. But unless supported with training and an increase in personnel, this politically correct approach is, in so many cases, unworkable and unmanageable for teachers, especially new ones.

Unless mainstream teachers are adequately trained and supported, learning for all students suffers, and we will continue to be plagued by "bad teachers."

Toward that end, I believe that *all* teachers should be trained in special education or receive at least some in-depth, longer-term training in this area. Not the drive-by knowledge that I received in my graduate program. With special-education students making up more than a tenth of all students nationwide—and a much higher percentage in low-income areas—special ed is now mainstream education. The techniques and insights of a well-trained special-ed teacher can be useful to any teacher every day.

In addition, I believe that teacher training should be less theoretical and more "clinical," hands-on and practical. Just as doctors train by doing rounds with experienced physicians and residencies at hospitals or clinics, teachers should have to train with seasoned pros for extended periods of time. The setting of the public school class is the ideal place to learn the how and why of everything from lesson plans to *shhh*ing gestures. Spend a year with a supportive, articulate practitioner like my state-trooper-grimacing friend Ms. Lyons, and you will be on the path to being not only a good teacher, but a damn good teacher.

Lesson 8: Discipline must be taken seriously.

At Latinate, Ms. P had set up a general reporting system based on plausible deniability. She tried hard to keep her fingerprints off anything negative—from manipulated data to classroom chaos. Whatever went wrong at the school was someone else's fault. Generally, a teacher's fault. Her dictate that teachers must handle all in-class behavior issues themselves was a good case in point. She promoted the school as a cathedral of learning populated by young scholars. If these scholars happened to be tossing each other over the desks or trying to stuff each other into classroom lockers, she wasn't to blame.

A swift, fair, and certain discipline system simply did not exist. It varied from class to class, teacher to teacher. There was a lot of tough talk about detention, but it really was discouraged by the administration, since it tied up administrators. So the kids often were released within minutes. Also, it was up to the individual teacher to make sure that the appropriate online data was input for detention and a parent was notified ahead of time. More serious behavior problems? The teacher should meet with a parent. All of this required even more time from the taxed teachers, so sending problematic students to detention was often even more problematic than the issue was worth, even if it was severe.

What about sending a disruptive kid out of the classroom when the problem started? At Latinate, only a very bad teacher would do that. Even I wasn't that bad.

Yet, I believe, that's what it would take. Pull disruptive kids out, and make discipline and behavior the hallmark of the school. Forbid cell phones. Don't merely put a cell-phone ban on the list of unenforced non-negotiables, but truly forbid them. I found that cell phones were the root of many in-class discipline and concentration problems.

Kids texting each other in class can spill out of digital communication and become a shouting—even shoving—match. Constantly checking messages that are forwarded around the room further erodes short attention spans. Even a good teacher has a hard time being more engaging than the newsfeed on Facebook.

New York City public schools that have security personnel tending metal detectors at the doorway can keep the phones out. In some cases, nearby bodegas or even entrepreneurs in curbside trucks hold the kids' phones for a dollar each during the school day. It can be a very lucrative, all-cash business. Some kids opt to leave their phones at home to avoid the cost. (Imagine that!) Schools that don't have a high probability of gun and knife violence aren't metal-detector equipped. Some of them avoid in-school cell phone problems by requiring the kids to secure their phones every day in tiny lockers by the front door that they can't access until the school day is over.

Violators receive swift, certain punishment such as suspension. And it works. Regularly reinforcing that swift, certain discipline is key, however. Latinate didn't have a metal detector, for example. But the no-phones non-negotiable was enforced randomly and irregularly, and teachers who attempted to enforce it didn't receive adequate backup from the administration, so it was, in effect, not a rule but a suggestion.

Close behind cell phones as a disruptive force were sugar highs and sugar crashes. Many kids came to school each day with a fistful of candy and sweetened iced tea, picked up at the bodega. The daily free, city-sponsored breakfast was hardly sugar-free; it was the same with lunch. Plus, Ms. P had the eighth graders peddling two-dollar candy bars to raise funds for their "senior" activities. This diet alone was enough to put many kids into disciplinary orbit.

I believe that sugary foods, drinks, and fund-raising products should be banned from public schools. I hate to come down against cupcakes and home-baked brownies, but if you ever had to handle a roomful of eighth graders freshly infused with icing, you too would insist on going sugar-free. It's important to teach our kids healthy habits, both inside and outside school, and this is a crucial place to start.

A principal who handles discipline problems at arm's length isn't a visionary leader. That person is a con artist. A school like Latinate can serve the students—especially the most promising students—by having rules that are backed by the certainty of discipline. The kids must *know* that if they act up there will be specific consequences ranging from being stuck in a SAVE room with a hard-ass dean to being suspended, even expelled. Otherwise, what leverage do we have with kids?

The rules need not be oppressively strict nor the punishments draconian. Instead, it all should be quite reasonable but *certain*. Without such a system, the only one benefitting is the principal, who is not responsible for disruptive students, and can blame any behavior problems and achievement issues on bad teachers.

Lesson 9: There must be a better way to evaluate teachers.

Like most people, I have no idea how police officers, firefighters, nurses, or trash collectors are evaluated on their job performance. Rating these workers—and publicizing their grades—has not become part of the national conversation. Maybe it will as data-driven accountability spreads. But until then, cops aren't blamed for our country's crime problems, firefighters for our safety problems, nurses for our health problems, or trash collectors for our environmental problems. So why are teachers being blamed for our education problems? There must be measures of performance along with some accountability that we can develop to effectively evaluate teachers. But what are they?

The students certainly are good indicators. Are they learning? Are they progressing? Is something magical happening with at least some of them? Or none at all? Some of what a teacher achieves probably can be displayed on an Excel spreadsheet as data. But so much of it can't. For that, peer, student, and principal reviews of performance can be useful. Outside observers, trained to do teacher evaluations based on criteria agreed to by all parties, might also play an effective role, as long as there is a system in place to ensure the observers are objectively selected and unbiased.

No system can be flawless, but right now, ours is failing, and it's getting worse. America's schools, school districts, cities, states, and federal departments use hundreds of different systems to determine teacher quality. It's not just important but crucial that we streamline these different methods into one comprehensive system. Teachers must be evaluated fairly and accurately on a number of different criteria by a number of objective parties. The goal shouldn't be punishment. It should be ensuring that our teachers receive the training and support they need to offer our kids the best education possible.

Lesson 10. Parents come in every variety.

"You tell me when to be here, and I will be here," Tiandra's mom said. "I will sit in the back of the classroom and make sure she behaves."

"I know you will," I told her. "That's why it probably won't be necessary."

"Well, you just call, and I will be here."

Tiandra's mom drove a bus for a living. Her shift started early in the morning and went until about 10:30, when she had a five-hour break before returning to work for the afternoon rush. This gave her plenty of time to keep an eye on Tiandra. If she works the same way she stays on her daughter, I know who should drive if the Navy SEALs ever conduct a mission by bus.

"Her brother is in college," Tiandra's mom told me one day. "That's where I want Tiandra, too."

In the meantime, her daughter was in the eighth grade at Latinate. And as Tiandra's mom knew, on a day-to-day basis, there were many distractions and roadblocks on her daughter's path to following in her brother's footsteps.

"In my forty-three years, I have seen what can go wrong, and I'm not going to let it happen to Tiandra," Tiandra's mom said in her clear, quick-cadence, single-breath way.

And when she turned from me and looked at her daughter,

saying, "Did you hear that, Tiandra?" I also could hear in her voice years of barking, "Step back. Make room for other passengers."

A tall, thin, pretty girl resembling a young Tyra Banks, Tiandra hadn't yet become the center of the boys' attention. Instead, she was deep in a circle of eighth-grade girls who wielded fierce tempers and acid tongues. The leader was Musica, a slightly overweight girl who was intelligent and a good reader, and who possessed a lightning-fast mind. She sometimes sat quietly and did her work, though more frequently, she acted out, sang, and talked. Yet anything touching on family or loss would bring her to tears.

I regularly threatened to call Musica's mother.

"You don't have her number," she would sneer. "Nobody does."

I made it a point to get the phone number, and Tiandra's mom put me in touch with several other moms, aunts, and grandmothers. One day, Musica was prancing around the back of the room during my lesson, a balloon stuffed under her shirt pretending she was pregnant.

"Look what Nestor gave me," she sang to the class, patting the maternity-worthy bulge.

"Musica," I said firmly from the front of the room. "I'm going to call your mother and tell her that you are running around pretending you have Nestor's baby."

"Ohhhhhhhhh," said the class.

"He don't have the number," Musica sang to her audience.

"2...1...2...7...6...7..." Before I could finish, she froze.

"That's my mother's work number! How did you get it?"

The next time I tried the number, however, it didn't work. And Musica was back to her usual antics.

Meanwhile, Tiandra's mom was in constant touch. And often waiting for her daughter outside the school in the afternoon.

Before long, Tiandra was doing her work and pushing back against the misbehavior of Musica.

"I prayed for this," Tiandra's mom told me.

"You also made it happen," I told her.

"Yes, I did," she said proudly.

When my article "Confessions of a Bad Teacher" appeared on Salon.com, some readers commented that the problems of Latinate and other high-needs schools could be traced to the parents. Bad parents. Or lack of any parents at all. There also were a couple mean-spirited comments along the lines of: "What do you expect from the offspring of such low-life characters?"

Perhaps some of the parents were low-life characters, as I had heard stories of drug-addled parents from other teachers. I found many parents, grandmothers, aunts, cousins, and siblings who clearly didn't want to have anything to do with Mr. Owens. Maybe they were low-life characters. Or maybe they were preoccupied with other equally important life struggles.

But it's important to note that while Tiandra's mom was the standout, she was hardly alone in her caring and attentiveness. Parent-teacher night brought almost 20 percent of my students' adult representatives, most coming directly from work, with some of the African and Dominican immigrant parents attending even though they didn't speak English. The parents were led to believe that Latinate was giving their kids an "Amazing!" education and all of the advantages. The parents were delighted to hear the words "scholars" and "college preparatory." The teachers' assurances, along with a constant barrage of jargon-laden material sent home from Ms. P (such as "The Principal's Newsletter"), underscored the upward educational rise of the children.

Much of this, of course, was pure theater, part of the pageant of today's successful school. These parents—many who were new to the country and most who didn't have any college experience—were easy marks. So when the Department of Education survey arrived in their mailbox asking them to evaluate their child's school, Latinate—and especially its founding principal—got high scores. Without this con, many parents would have done much more. They would have pushed their kids harder, and been more demanding and stricter about in-school behavior. But the overall impression they received was that things were going well.

When things didn't go well, however, the issues often were beyond what the parents could handle. When faced with a kid with special needs (ADHD, just for starters) or a kid under the influence of the likes of the very troubled Natasha, these parents were overwhelmed. They didn't know where to turn for real help, and neither did I.

In contrast to these well-meaning but paralyzed parents were those who knew exactly what to do—blame somebody. There was a small group that viewed everything through the lens of an aggrieved party. They were always victims and there was no way to please them. Yet for all their conspiracy theories, they didn't recognize that Ms. P was perpetrating a scam.

Of course, poor parenting skills know no economic or demographic boundaries. The "helicopter parents" who hover over every move their children make are micromanaging their kids into helplessness, resentfulness, or a sense that only what the parent thinks is important is important. And, as I see in my daughter's public school, some parents refuse to believe their children are at fault in anything from bad behavior to failing grades—and *somebody else* has to be at fault.

When the dust settles and the students at last take their seats, no matter how good or bad the parents, in today's school, it's the teacher—and typically only the teacher—who is held accountable for the kids' performance.

WHAT WE CAN DO

It's making a difference in the world that prevents me from ever giving up.
—Deborah Meier, legendary teacher and founder
of the modern small-school movement

I WAS STAGGERED BY the myriad of problems I encountered at Latinate, but in the end, I wasn't disheartened. If anything, I've been energized by the experience. From the day I left the New York City public school system, I have worked to bring this story to light and provide even a small counterweight to the powerful forces that are disenfranchising both our neediest children and students everywhere with the current misguided ideas of school reform. It's my way of giving back to my students.

My quest started with the article on Salon.com, continued with this book, and will go on, in the hope of educating and stirring the indignation of parents and taxpayers who will stand up for the kids and fight the cheating, the finger-pointing, and the bad-teacher witch hunts in their schools, so we can actually create effective change for American students. This is everyone's problem—and everyone can help, somehow.

Here are some groups, people, and actions that you can connect with to be part of the solution.

Parents Across America

A great first step is to join an education-focused organization that has both local and national presence. One nonprofit I recommend is Parents Across America, a nationwide grassroots group that describes itself as "committed to bringing the voice of public school parents—and common sense—to local, state, and national education debates."

Founded a decade ago by parents and activists from around the country, the group uses its website, e-newsletter, and social media to keep its members up to date on educational issues and provide the facts and tactics that parents need to affect change on a local level. Among the wisdom put forth by PAA is its mission statement, a brilliant distillation of what works and doesn't work in public education. Here are some highlights:

What Works

Proven Reforms: We support the expansion of sensible, research-based reforms, such as pre-K programs, full-day kindergarten, small classes, parent involvement, strong, experienced teachers, a well-rounded curriculum, and evaluation systems that go beyond test scores.

Sufficient and Equitable Funding: Resources do matter, especially when invested in programs that have been proven to work.

What Doesn't Work

Privatization: A strong public education system is fundamental to our democracy. We oppose efforts to privatize public education through the expansion of charters, vouchers, or other privately run programs at the expense of regular public schools.

High-Stakes Testing: Excessive reliance on standardized exams narrows the curriculum, promotes teaching to the test, and leads to unfair and unreliable evaluations of students, teachers, and schools.

Ignoring Poverty: The nation's educational "crisis" is made worse by the widening gap between rich and poor. Along with investing in our schools, we should also be investing in families.

Join this group, and you are linked with like-minded people who bring the abuses of school reform to the national stage. Not only has PAA demonstrated at political conventions, but the group has also called out the media when they lose their objectivity and swoon over the latest teacher-bashing, public-school-closing visionary leader. In addition, local chapters and affiliated organizations take on issues at the state and community level. The members' passion for and knowledge of public education will inspire you in any battles you choose to fight. (Visit ParentsAcrossAmerica.org.)

Save Our Schools

Talk about a call to action! Save Our Schools (SOS) came together in 2010 with the idea of fighting the attacks on public education with a very powerful and time-honored all-American tool: a march on Washington. Led by educators from the elementary school to the university level, as well as social-justice activists, the group converged on the nation's capital in July 2011 with thousands of participants taking part in demonstrations, a rally, and an issues-oriented conference. Rebelling against attacks on public education and public school teachers, SOS frames the issues in language that echoes socialist revolutionaries, using terms such as "struggle," "resistance," and "unity."

But whatever your politics, SOS's energy is irresistible, and the group has a real understanding of the issues involved in saving our public schools and ensuring a better and equal education for all. SOS defines the problem succinctly:

> Teachers and their unions are being blamed for the failings of the system. A mania for testing is driving curriculum, instruction, and funding. There is a concerted, well-financed effort to privatize all of public education. Public schools and teachers are being evaluated and punished on the basis of their students' standardized test scores. Neighborhood schools, which are the most valuable assets in under-resourced communities, are being closed and replaced with privately run charter schools. National standards, curriculum, and testing regimens are being imposed top-down by corporate-style reformers and the Department of Education to the detriment of children learning.

Among the superstar writers and thinkers involved with SOS is Jonathan Kozol, a long-time advocate for the poor whose quote opens the previous chapter. He is the author of many highly influential books on education, including the brilliant and shocking *The Shame of the Nation: Restoration of Apartheid Schooling in America; Savage Inequalities: Children in America's Schools;* and most recently, *Fire in the Ashes: Twenty-Five Years among the Poorest Children in America.* No one speaks as articulately and movingly about the lives of children caught in poverty. Kozol brings them to life and makes the reader not merely want to affect change but *demand* it. Truly, a powerful voice.

Another powerful voice deeply involved with SOS is legendary educator Deborah Meier (whose quote opens this chapter). A former kindergarten teacher, she is widely considered the founder of the modern small-school movement. Her successes with a progressive approach to education have earned her numerous honors, including a MacArthur Fellowship. Her books include *In Schools We Trust: Creating Communities of Learning in an Era of Testing and Standardization.* Though first published in 2002, it remains quite relevant in terms of insight and action. In addition to her website (DeborahMeier.com), she has a blog, "Bridging Differences," on the *Education Week* site (blogs.edweek.org/edweek/Bridging -Differences), where along with Pedro Noguera—author and director of the Metropolitan Center for Urban Education—she discusses issues involving schools, teachers, and students.

With top-level intellectual horsepower and a strong call to action (Yes, the marches will continue), SOS became a national presence virtually overnight. Though the group's language sometimes seems extreme, the severity of the problem America is facing is extreme, too. Visit the website (SaveOurSchoolsMarch.org) for a concise and accurate take on the issues. The site also has actions you can take right now—from signing online petitions to joining parents nationwide who opt out of high-stakes testing for their children.

Diane Ravitch, PhD

When it comes to deft analysis of what passes for school reform, no one is better than Diane Ravitch (whose quote opens this book). Historian of education, educational policy analyst, and research professor at New York University, Ravitch is the author of numerous books, including the 2010 best-seller *The Death and Life of the Great American School System: How Testing and Choice Are Undermining Education.* That powerful book is just the start. Her blog, dianeravitch.net, is the go-to spot for deflating the latest "great idea." Updated constantly—many times each day—the blog is more than a discussion; it's a brilliant call to action.

Ravitch once was U.S. Assistant Secretary of Education. With luck and pressure, perhaps the President will do the right thing and get her involved in policy once again. In the meantime, on her website (DianeRavitch.com), she offers some ideas on what we can do (in addition to joining Parents Across America, with which she is involved). Her suggestions are straightforward, ranging from writing to elected officials to running for a spot on the school board. But Ravitch is absolutely correct—this kind of action can make a profound difference.

Act Locally

In fact, most of us can have the most impact close to home, right in our own communities. It doesn't get more grassroots or important than helping individual students. Mentor a kid, if you can. Children throughout the country need as many adults as possible in their lives supporting the idea that education is important. Becoming a mentor shows a kid that he or she is personally important enough to have an adult helping out. Your best bet is to connect with guidance counselors and parent organizations at your local schools, which also can offer ideas for how you can help. If your local school system doesn't have a mentoring program, offer to set one up.

Can't make that commitment? Give a teacher a gift certificate for supplies and instructional materials. With today's budget cuts, a classroom-level gift can be a godsend. Do it the old-fashioned way with a gift card in an envelope, or join the millions who do it online at DonorsChoose.org.

The brainchild of Charles Best, a teacher at a Bronx high school, DonorsChoose.org lists specific projects at various public schools. (The teachers set up the projects on the site.) You pick which gets your money. The site is so engaging that it's easy to spend hours browsing the thousands of projects as you perform your own classroom-level philanthropy. So far, more than $100 million has been donated to support hundreds of thousands of public school projects.

What makes this so appealing is not just the specificity of your gift, but that you know the class receives it. DonorsChoose.org uses the contributions to the individual project to buy the supplies for the project and ships the stuff directly to the schools. You get a line-item budget, a photograph of the project, and a letter from the teacher. Give enough, and the kids will write you, too.

Above all, don't simply believe what the headlines say about our educational system. When it comes to public education, the truth is often—make that *usually*—far from what you read in the media. Talk to real students and real teachers. When the reports and reality don't mesh, speak up. Be a gadfly at board of education meetings. Write letters to the editor of the local newspaper. Meet with school officials. You will have clout. You will make a difference. Don't let your schools squander precious time and money on empty promises and quick fixes disguised by fancy words and lofty ideals. Our children and the future of our country don't need this theater. They need *education*.

EPILOGUE

T HE STUDENTS, TEACHERS, AND staff of Latinate moved
through and out of the school in such large numbers and
so quickly that it often felt more like a bus station than a stable
institution. As difficult as it was to keep track of them and keep
in touch, here are the latest reports available to me as this book
went to press:

Between the time I left Latinate and when the next school year was about to begin...

- Ms. Lyons transferred to another South Bronx middle
  school where she teaches science. "My God answers
  prayers," she said.
- Ms. Patel retired the instant she clocked twenty-five years in
  the System. In retirement, she teaches literature at a college
  in New Jersey. "It is wonderful," she said. "I love it! The
  students really care and really do the work because they are
  spending their own money to take the class."
- Ms. Perker received a Satisfactory rating from Ms. P and continued her special-ed career for a second year at Latinate.
- Mr. Rodriquez received a Satisfactory rating, continued his
  quest for tenure, and continued to coach the Archery Club.
- Ms. Nenza and Mr. Steinman received Satisfactory ratings
  from Ms. P and stayed for a second year.

- The dean moved to another school after receiving an Unsatisfactory rating from Ms. P.
- The guidance counselor found a position at a private school after receiving an Unsatisfactory rating from Ms. P.
- A tenured Spanish teacher received an Unsatisfactory rating from Ms. P but stayed at the school.
- The tenured physical-education teacher received an Unsatisfactory rating from Ms. P but stayed at the school.
- The payroll secretary received an Unsatisfactory rating from Ms. P but stayed at the school.
- A senior administrator abruptly quit mid-year after receiving an Unsatisfactory rating from Ms. P and handed her keys to the custodian on her way out.

As the next school year got under way...

- Ms. P and the assistant principal were escorted from the school by Department of Education officials, following a scandal involving falsifying records of student progress. An assistant principal from another Bronx school was appointed principal at Latinate.

And before long...

- The lead teacher moved to another school.
- Ms. Adebayo, the tenured science teacher with a law degree and a strong Nigerian accent, who had received yet another Unsatisfactory rating from Ms. P before she was fired, left Latinate. She now practices law.
- Mr. Bookbinder, the talkative, 1970s-style English teacher who had received yet another Unsatisfactory rating from Ms. P, was brought up on charges of "incompetence" by the Department of Education. Relieved of classroom responsibilities, he spent

his days sitting in the school's second-floor office, collecting his pay while awaiting adjudication of his case.

The kids? Santos, the bright, industrious eighth grader, moved to a small Bronx public high school for ninth grade and beyond. Though better regarded than Latinate, Santos' new school was not one of the "elite" city high schools, where the students are overwhelmingly white and Asian. The other kids, for the most part, remained at Latinate and continued, year after year, to move up from grade to grade toward graduation. In other words, many of them, regrettably, were swallowed by the System.

As for me, when it became clear that my New York City teaching career would unfortunately be coming to a premature, U-based end, I returned to publishing. I'm now the editor in chief of a newspaper company that publishes sixteen weekly papers. My new working conditions—a private office, a staff, and no need to lock up my lunch and computer—are obviously far better than those at Latinate Institute.

But I had a gnawing sense of disappointment. I'd invested nearly two years of time, energy, and graduate school tuition, and I'd failed in what I'd set out to accomplish. I also felt terrible about leaving the kids—especially my ninth-grade writers. I thought long and very hard about many different ways to help them further. Ultimately, I decided the most important and effective way would be to share not only my story, but their stories as well—to make people aware of this issue and encourage them to solve it. By doing so, I hope that in some way I help "my kids" and the myriad others like them.

BIBLIOGRAPHY

Bill & Melinda Gates Foundation. "Empowering Effective Teachers: Strategies for Implementing Reforms." Seattle: Gates Foundation, 2010. Accessed December 26, 2012. http://www.gatesfoundation .org/united-states/Documents/empowering-effective-teachers -empowering-strategy.pdf.

Bush, Jeb. "Lead or Get Out of the Way on Schools." *Politico*, August 4, 2011. Accessed December 26, 2012. http://www.politico.com/news /stories/0811/60651.html.

Center for Research on Education Outcomes (CREDO) atStanford University. "Multiple Choice: Charter School Performance in 16 States." 2009. Accessed January 12, 2013. http://credo.stanford.edu/reports /MULTIPLE_CHOICE_CREDO.pdf.

Coalition for Psychology in Schools and Education. *Report on the Teacher Needs Survey*. Washington, D.C.: American Psychological Association, Center for Psychology in Schools and Education, August 2006. Accessed January 2, 2013. http://www.apa.org/ed/schools /coalition/teachers-needs.pdf.

Comprehensive School Reform Program Office. Office of Elementary and Secondary Education. U.S. Department of Education. Scientifically Based Research and the Comprehensive School Reform (CSR) Program. Washington, D.C.: U.S. Department of Education, 2002. Accessed December 26, 2012. http://www2.ed.gov /programs/compreform/guidance/appendc.pdf.

Coppin, Joyce R. "Rating Pedagogical Staff Members." Brooklyn: New York City Department of Education, Office of Appeals and Reviews, 2002. Accessed December 26, 2012. http://www.uft.org/files/attachments/rating-pedagogical-staff-members.pdf.

Ewing, John. "Mathematical Intimidation: Driven by the Data." *Notices of the American Mathematical Society*, May 2011. Accessed December 26, 2012. http://www.ams.org/notices/201105/rtx110500667p.pdf.

Foote, Mary Q., Andrew Brantlinger, Hanna N. Haydar, Beverly Smith, and Lidia Gonzalez. "Are We Supporting Teacher Success: Insights From an Alternative Route Mathematics Teacher Certification Program for Urban Public Schools." *Education and Urban Society*, May 2011. Accessed January 13, 2013. http://eus.sagepub.com/content/43/3/396.abstract?patientinform-links=yes&legid=speus;43/3/396.

Grissom, Jason A. and Lael Keiser. "The Impact of Principal Race on Teachers." (Report 09-2011.) University of Missouri Columbia, Institute of Public Policy, 2011. Accessed December 26, 2012. http://ipp.missouri.edu/files/ipp/attachments/09-2011_impact_of_principal_race_on_teachers.pdf.

Hemphill, Clara. "Public Schools That Work." In *City Schools: Lessons from New York*, edited by Diane Ravitch and Joseph P. Viteritti, 45–64. Baltimore: The Johns Hopkins Press, 2000.

Kleinsorge, Christy, and Lynne M. Covitz. "Impact of Divorce on Children: Developmental Considerations." *Pediatrics in Review* 33(2012): 147–155. Accessed December 26, 2012. http://pedsinreview.aappublications.org/content/33/4/147.extract.

Kozol, Jonathon. *Fire in the Ashes: Twenty-Five Years among the Poorest Children in America*. New York: Crown Publishers, 2012.

Kozol, Jonathon. *Savage Inequalities: Children in America's Schools*. New York: HarperCollins Publishers, 1992.

Kozol, Jonathon. *The Shame of the Nation: The Restoration of Apartheid Schooling in America*. New York: Crown Publishers, 2005.

Meier, Deborah. *In Schools We Trust: Creating Communities of Learning in an Era of Testing and Standardization*. Boston: Beacon Press, 2002.

MetLife. *The MetLife Survey of the American Teacher: Teachers, Parents, and the Economy*. New York: MetLife Inc., March 2012. Accessed January 2, 2013. https://www.metlife.com/assets/cao/contributions /foundation/american-teacher/MetLife-Teacher-Survey-2011.pdf.

National Commission on Teaching and America's Future. "The High Cost of Teacher Turnover." Washington, D.C.: National Commission on Teaching and America's Future, 2007. Accessed December 26, 2012. http://nctaf.org/wp-content/uploads/2012/01/NCTAF -Cost-of-Teacher-Turnover-2007-policy-brief.pdf.

Ravitch, Diane. *The Death and Life of the Great American School System: How Testing and Choice Are Undermining Education*. New York: Basic Books, 2010.

Ronfeldt, Matthew, Susanna Loeb, and James Wyckoff. "How Teacher Turnover Harms Student Achievement." National Bureau of Economic Research Working Paper No. 17176, June 2011. Accessed January 12, 2013. http://www.nber.org/papers/w17176.

Tennessee Department of Education. "TVAAS: Tennessee Value-Added Assessment System." Nashville: Tennessee Department of Education, 2010. Accessed December 26, 2012. http://www.tn.gov /education/assessment/doc/TVAAS_Elem-Middle-High.pdf.

U.S. Department of Education. Institute of Education Sciences. National Center for Education Statistics. "America's Charter Schools: Results from the NAEP 2003 Pilot Study." Washington, D.C.: National Center for Education Statistics, 2004. Accessed December 26, 2012. http://nces.ed.gov/pubsearch/pubsinfo.asp?pubid=2005456.

Willingham, Daniel T. "Why Does Family Wealth Affect Learning?" *American Educator*, Spring 2012. Accessed December 26 2012. http:// www.aft.org/pdfs/americaneducator/spring2012/Willingham.pdf.

ACKNOWLEDGMENTS

A huge "Thank you!" to my inspired, energetic, and all-around wonderful agent, Nena Madonia, and to the incomparable Jan Miller at Dupree Miller & Associates.

My editor, the brilliantly sharp Stephanie Bowen at Sourcebooks, Inc., proves the power of questions.

Sarah Hepola, my editor at Salon.com, helped a bad teacher make good.

The courageous, prolific Diane Ravitch is a role model who keeps me typing.

My wife, Demetria, and my daughter, Aidan, provide real-world inspiration.

Randy Steele deserves credit for bearing with me.

Peter Crescenti, Marta Genovese, and Caroline Applequist I thank for their kindness.

Thanks in advance to Angela Susan Anton and Michael Castonguay for their enthusiasm and support.

The writers in the ninth-grade writing workshop often made magic with eighty words. I hope they continue to do so.

ABOUT THE AUTHOR

J OHN OWENS IS A writer, editor, publishing executive, and former teacher. A frequent commentator and guest on national TV and radio programs, John lives with his wife, Demetria, and their daughter, Aidan, in New York. Reach him at jowens@thebadteacher.com.